GUST

Gust

POEMS

GREG ALAN BROWNDERVILLE

TRIQUARTERLY BOOKS

NORTHWESTERN UNIVERSITY PRESS

EVANSTON, ILLINOIS

TriQuarterly Books
Northwestern University Press
www.nupress.northwestern.edu

Printed in the United States of America

10 9 8 7 6 5 4 3 2 1

Library of Congress Cataloging-in-Publication Data

Brownderville, Greg Alan.
    Gust : poems / Greg Alan Brownderville.
      p. cm.
    Poems, some previously published.
    Includes bibliographical references.
    ISBN 978-0-8101-5221-2 (pbk. : alk. paper)
    I. Title.
  PS3602.R728G87 2011
  811'.6—dc22

                                                    2011015571

∞ The paper used in this publication meets the minimum require-
ments of the American National Standard for Information Sciences—
Permanence of Paper for Printed Library Materials, ANSI Z39.48-1992.

This book is dedicated to Brother Langston, Sister Law,
and the Sycamore Six

Contents

PART I. *Press In*

PART II. *The Wild Yonder Blues*

PART III. *Becoming Hot Tamale Charlie*

PART IV. *Ghosts*

Acknowledgments

My thanks to the editors of these periodicals for publishing versions of the following poems.

Arkansas Review: "The Cold Tile Blues" and "Goblin Song"

Birmingham Poetry Review: "Carlo Flunks the Seventh Grade," "From a Nationally Televised Press Conference Starring the Poetic Sheriff, Joseph Kilpatrick Conway, After a van Gogh Painting Is Stolen from a Little Rock Exhibit and Recovered in Monroe County," "Hot Tamale Charlie Speaks of Rabbit Ice," "The Magic of Song," and "Tableland at Zero"

Country Dog Review: "A Swiss Vintner in the Land of Muscadines"

First Things: "The Mailbox"

Gravy: "Carlo on the Hog Slaughter" and "The Cold Tile Blues"

The HyperTexts: "Marble to Flesh, Flesh to Marble"

Journal of the Association for Research on Mothering: "All of This Only Fifty Miles from the Former Home of L. Frank Baum, Creator of *The Wonderful Wizard of Oz*"

Kritya: "Firecrackers," "The Love Song of Jephthah's Daughter," and "A Welder's New Year's Eve"

Measure: "The Palm Tree Soliloquies" and "Telephoning"

Oxford American: "Arkansas Blacks," "Honey Behind the Sun," "Last Song for Brother Langston," and "Waking Up in Baghdad"

Prairie Schooner: "Driftwood," "Lord, Make Me a Sheep," and "The Mysterious Bar-B-Q Grill of Turkey Scratch, Arkansas"

The Raintown Review: "Hot Tamale Charlie Sings of a Player's Heartbreak" and "Soul-Selling Ritual"

I am grateful to *Prairie Schooner* for presenting me its 2010 Jane Geske Award for "Driftwood," "Lord, Make Me a Sheep," and "The Mysterious Bar-B-Q Grill of Turkey Scratch, Arkansas" and to *New Millennium Writings* for awarding me a poetry prize for "A Soldier Gets Home." My thanks to *The Missouri Review* for naming me the winner of its 2011 Voice-Only Poetry contest for "Sex and Pentecost" and to my brother, Eric, for engineering and producing the winning audio recording.

Special thanks to my writing teachers: Beth Ann Fennelly, Gary Short, Ann Fisher-Wirth, Tom Franklin, Barry Hannah, Daniel Anderson, Andrew Hudgins, Mary Jo Salter, Dave Smith (who has made Johns Hopkins feel like my second M.F.A. home), Johnny "Road O' Burnin' Rum" Wink, and Rod Kidwell. I am a fortunate beneficiary of their wise and candid counsel.

Many thanks to Wyatt Prunty, Cheri Bedell Peters, and all the other fine folks with the Sewanee Writers' Conference, through which so many blessings have come into my life; and to the Nebraska Summer Writers Conference—especially to Hilda Raz for helping me organize this book. A heartfelt word of gratitude goes to the Porter Fund Literary Prize—especially to its cofounders, Phillip McMath and Jack Butler.

I am much obliged to Jack Barbera, Tim Earley, Ivo Kamps, Donald Kartiganer, Larry Lowman, Isaac Mwase (who gave me the gift of Shona), Jerry Nelson, Bobby Rea, Gregory Schirmer, Danielle Sellers, Alex Taylor, Anne-Marie Thompson, Hicks Wogan, and Linda Wyman. Special thanks to Alan Shapiro, whose kindness was essential to the fulfillment of this project. Finally, I am grateful to my extraordinary family—especially to my parents, Pamela Jane and Alton Brownderville; Eric Brownderville; the late Edrie Molena Woodall; and Stacy, Randy, Calfskin, and Katelyn Ohlde—for their tremendous love and support.

GUST

FIRECRACKERS

My childhood favorite was the one that popped
high in the air and dropped a little plastic paratrooper.
Hard to see and harder to catch,
it drifted toward the cotton patch amid a burst
of blue, electrical confetti.
As blizzard-thick mosquitoes mesmerized me
with their hum, the paratrooper landed in the loam,
magnificently mine—like burning words
I'd aimed at heaven, come back as a poem.

military number that parachutes from airplanes

soil - like sand + clay

Establish setting
Past - childhood
Present - poet

I

PRESS IN

DARK CORNER

1

Me and Sparrel Rance were friends
ever since they clipped our unbiblical cords.
Side by side as babies,
we rode our mamas' cotton sacks,
and later worked from can't to can't ?
together in the fields.
Soon as Aubrey, Sparrel's brother,
got old enough to shadow us,
he made it three,
and Dark Corner, Arkansas,
had never seen such devilment.

2

Our fifteenth summer,
men and boys both, me and Sparrel
lit a fire below a rotten tupelo
and smoked out the bees.
We sawed the tree down, stole the hive,
and trucked it home along a path as wavy as a panther tail.
We cut the comb
in little waffly squares to go in every jar.
That was the awfullest amount of honey—
filled up two number three washtubs
like we took a bath in. After we got it all canned,
a few jars had some live bees in them.

We were sucking honey off the comb,
and Sparrel asked if I believed in ghosts.
I told him I would have to think about it.
He said one night when he was six, a shadowman
with an ankly cypress branch for a cane
shambled in the house
and lifted Aubrey off his corn shucks,
held him for a spell, and said, "Are you dead yet?"

3

Me and Sparrel went frog gigging
one night. I held the light.
Where the swamp was loggy
and we couldn't pass,   *dialect*
you'd a thought bluegrass <u>done gone</u> metal,
way he worked that banjo of a chain saw.

Gar passed the boat
like black submarines.
We floated, listening to locusts, tree frogs, panthers—
thought we saw a bull shark up from the Gulf.
As the moon slipped under cloud cover
like a scared face,
drumfish took to drumming.
"Listen," Sparrel whispered.
"Listen to that drum—
it's like a stuttering heart."

I was paddling, not to get somewhere
but just for pleasure, working that lazy water,
and Sparrel said, "I swear
it was a wet tornado."
Said it a little too loud, like I was arguing.

"If I'd a jumped in, we both might a died.
I should a tried."
I told him he was talking crazy.
He said, "God won't save me—
he's doing me just like I done Aubrey."
Said sleep was a strong woman
but couldn't take him anymore.
Every night he stuck to his covers,
doused with sweat,
seeing Aubrey spit and flail and bob loud-eyed
like a Holy Roller getting baptized.
"One night," he said, "I threw my sheet off
and the demons come a-swishing in
chilly through my pores.
Next day I seen Jesus in overalls,
nibbling a ground-cherry.
He moseyed off into the tall cotton,
saying, 'See you in the funny papers.'"

4

This Monday at the market,
I spied a jar of raw local honey.
The comb was like a box of shells.
I thought of Sparrel Rance,
them eyes of his
like a kitten's not all the way open yet.
Late that man-child summer,
he fired a goose gun
at the stuttering drum in his chest
and left me,
left me a chain-saw banjo
and the need to truck with ghosts.

symbols: music instruments

youth
bees
frogs

Jesus
demons / ghosts
death – suicide,
friend

narrator alive
setting

9

Dirt-stopped, eary mussel shells were strewn
across alluvium jigsawed by the sun.
Barefoot, I waited, saw Jack Langston dunk
all comers in the Cache. God's champion.
Tall cypress knees loomed gray along the bank
like tombstones. As the line shrank,

words from "Jesus on the Mainline" rang
inside my head. (Sister Lila had sung
a couple rounds to start the ceremony.)
Call him up, rolling off a Southern tongue,
sounded like "call them up," reminding me
of Uncle Paul, of all I couldn't be

now that I was Langston's kind of Christian.
Tangly red hair like dodder in the sun,
Paul taught me how to call them up: He stole
his mama's antique hand-crank telephone—
a little generator, powerful
enough to be our magic fishing reel.

With rubber seats and boots we'd float the Cache,
cathedral-quiet if not for chirp or splash.
Mirrored dimly in the river's brown,
tupelos towered—cypress, gum, and ash.
We'd hook two twelve-gauge wires up to the phone
and drop them in the water twelve feet down.

Finally, when I was twelve, my uncle said,
"Here, man this winder—you ain't no little kid."

The fish lived through the shock but couldn't swim
for minutes, only float. I cranked like mad.
As Paul took hold of the dip net, here they came:
flathead, blue cat, buffalo, and bream . . .

It was time. My feet went clean invisible
and read the riverbed's treacherous Braille.
Langston covered my nose and mouth with white,
then braced my back and said, "Surrender all."
In a wet rush I felt my blood ignite
and shivered as I rose electrified.

ode to the South

youth
fish
death - fish
narrator aln
setting

SOUL-SELLING RITUAL

I make fire underneath an iron pot
and kill a cat nothing but black on its back,
skin it and boil it like the two-head said—
"Stare in a looking glass and run them cat bones
cross your tongue, one by one, till your reflection
disappear like a snakehead in the river.
That's when the Devil got your soul, old boy."

Next thing I know, I'm naked as the mange
and scrabbling in wet weeds by a blue shack.
Peacocks laughing, I laugh back, and pie pans
go changalanga in the cherry tree—
scarecrow tambourines. I kill the scarecrow,
steal his garb, and walk into the sky,
through a giant crystal tepee made of sunrays.

birds
cat
death-cat
devil
setting

In glimmering coils tuba-serpents beg,
  gaping their massive mouths
    to gulp the lunar egg.

Trombonists blow their melodies cheek tight
  and loose them like balloons
    untied and yellowy bright.

In streaming sound-confetti the dead arrive
  to claim this bead-strung city
    as their afterlife.

> *Baby's in the king cake*
> *God and the Devil one*
> *Deep down in New Orleans*
> *Honey behind the sun*

serpents
God
Devil
death
setting

Sister Law, a one-hundred-year-old preacher woman
and folk sculptor, walks to Cache River. Cypress knees
gather like silent monks around her. A daughter
of the forest and the river, she's at peace
among her holy men. Kneeling beside the water,
speckled with red haws and tea colored from leaf tannin,
she waits for driftwood. Her first find looks like a rabbit
in blurry midair stride, the next like fighting bears,
a third like her young face not yet crosshatched with years.
She lets them go. Breathing to still her imagination,
she knows the hardest thing to make now is the habit
of saying amen to the river, amen, amen.

older
not personal
inanimate

mystical

MAWU NAMES HER CHIEF ASSISTANT

Mawu, the dreaming Dahomean goddess,
escorted little Legba, her sly son,
through the yam garden. "I will bless
the new moons in your eyes with mystic vision,"
she said, "your hands with power. Human beings will honor
the dog, your totem beast;
worship in white, your ritual color;
and serve you oil and cornmeal cakes, your sacred feast.

"I will teach you the magic alphabet,
my deepest secret, and every evening write
beautiful poems about our planet—
mail to the dwellers of earth, to activate
their days and destinies." She smiled. "I am naming you
the cosmic carrier, next
to me the mightiest god of Voudou."
Sniggering, Legba thought, *Me tamper with the text.*

Good v Evil
Mawu   Legba
not personal
mystical

Fishermen lift their question marks from the lake
  in sudden rain. The clean horizon line,
a perfect moon, and its reflection make
    an obelus, a great division sign.
By the shore, I walk this glistening road alone—
  singing, against the wind's delirious keening,
    of the glad primal iamb. Divine breath,
  by wizardry of words, gave life to man
to complicate the tale. In the beginning
    was poetry. Then God invented death.

There were shadows, there were shivering and prayer.
  Tatterdemalions crammed inside a cave,
we smelled of our kill and richly of our maker.
    The firelight deemed us lovely, fit to save.
I could reforest Eden with a phrase,
  declare the cursive honeysuckle law,
    he thought, but easy mercy would have marred
  his poem, and he refused to compromise,
too proud to play the deus ex machina.
    How can I save my creatures—and my art?

My god, I feel him live—I feel him die.
  Arrows of rain. A lightning claw takes hold
of a leafless tree to shake hands in the sky.
    Some strange white thing, as if the gush of road
were a gentle river, makes a mad descent
  through blue-gray light and crashes, bleeds, transforms.

Gravity-panicked at the pavement's edge,
the bird is a book flapping in the wind.
Tomorrow crazed black flies will come in swarms,
characters loose and hungry for a page.

birds   poetry
flies   tale
God

LORD, MAKE ME A SHEEP

1

[handwritten: telephone]

Brother Langston's sermon over, we all stood.
Every head bowed, every eye closed.
A flannel-shirted lumberjack of a deacon named Joe Paul James
was bawling and squalling as usual:
"O Lowered, Jayzus, Lowered, move in our midst, Lowered."

Brother Langston said, "I don't keer *[handwritten: dialect]*
if you're a sinner man or woman or a holy saint of God—
come on, people, press in!
Get in under the spout where the glow-ree's coming out!
I want to see a hundred percent in this altar."

My older brother Eric knew the roving prayer warriors
had him on their Holy Ghost Hit List.
Had he stayed put, they might have come to his seat
and made a scene of wooing him back to the Lord.

(Or worse. One time, when a fifteen-year-old boy
ignored an altar call, an elder called him out by name,
said he had committed The Unpardonable Sin,
said he could pull his hair out in the altar
from "now till doomsday" but God
would never have him, never save him.)

So Eric eased up front and knelt
on a pew of knotty pine in the second row,
hoping to go unnoticed—a foolish move
that made him all the more conspicuous,
a timid sinner boy running from the Lord.

He bowed his head on folded forearms, and could smell
the Strawberry-Watermelon Hubba Bubba on his trapped breath.
The voice of Sister Lou, our piano player,
floated across the church—*Swing low, sweet chariot . . .*

Then a firm, vibrating hand
gripped the back of Eric's head like a gearshift.

It was Joe Paul James.
He bawled in a creepy, weepy falsetto,
"Make him a sheep, Lowered, make him a sheeeeeeeep."
On "sheeeeeeeep" Joe Paul hit a spooky minor note
like stormy winds that rattle windows, open and slam doors.

Eric, not a Bible buff, had no clue
what the goal of Joe Paul's prayer could be
except to turn him into a sheep.

Literally.

While Joe Paul was slobbering
through the same prayer over and over
("Make him a sheep, Lowered, make him a sheeeeeeeep!"),
Eric lifted up his head and cried out,
"BAAAAAAAA! BAAAAAAAA!"

The church fell gravely quiet,
and Joe Paul withdrew his hands and backed away
as if Eric were a holdup artist or a wolf,
anything but a sheep.
Eric stood up and sauntered back to his pew,
sat down beside me, and whispered,
"There's some world-class kooks in this church, I'm here to tell you."
A few folks flashed Eric V-browed frowns,
but most people, our parents among them,
tried to act as though nothing had happened.

Soon, Brother Langston asked everyone to stand.
After making a few announcements, he said, as always,
"Let's love the Lord and be dismissed,"
as if the alternative were to love Satan and stick around.

2

Sister Lou played piano
like a crazed novelist
at a magical typewriter.

She was a first-rate shouter.
When she sang, the Spirit blessed
the church, falling like manna

from heaven, sweet to the tongue.
One Sunday evening, Lou
broke out in the holy cackle.

(She must have been half grackle—
that caw, those shimmers of blue
in her black hair.) Her song,

They that wait upon the Lord
Shall renew their strength.
They shall mount up with wings . . . ,

melted to blissful moaning.
My coat a quilt beneath
the pews, I rubbed the hard

swirls of gum stuck above me
as if caressing nipples,
tuning in wild she-cries.

20

I closed my dreaming eyes.
Bathsheba came in ripples
to ride me, rev me, love me.

3

We found cold breakfast under Reynolds Wrap
and sat down in the kitchen by ourselves.
Upstairs, a vacuum's dying fall and then
the ever-louder plunks of Mama's feet.

Eric had smoked kind bud the night before
and left some evidence, an orange package,
in the fifth pocket of his jeans. That morning,
prepping the laundry, she'd discovered it.
She came into the room and slapped that pack
of Zig-Zag rolling papers on the table.

"You got some tall explaining to do, son."

Chewing, he said, "I'm glad you found that thing.
What is it anyway?"

                    "Don't give me that,"
she said. "You know exactly what it is."

He spread some mayhaw jelly on yellow toast
and said, "I saw it lying in the street
last night at the blues fest and thought it was
a pack of Chinese chewing gum. I picked
it up to take a look and didn't want
to litter, so I stuck it in my pocket."
The lie seemed too smooth in the telling,
too quirky to be anything but the truth.

Or maybe Mama needed to believe.
Months later, she found a box of Eric's ganja
paraphernalia in a dresser drawer.
That day, he smiled and said, "Greg, I get all
the righteous disapproval around here
because my sins're the kind you find in boxes.
But truth be known, you're further gone than I am."

He was right. Next to my apostasies
his beery Friday nights, boys being boys,
would have seemed harmless, almost cute. Those years
he spent flashing a fake ID and guzzling
till he was fucked up like a snake in a lawn mower,
bumbling with bra straps on a grass-stained quilt,

I waded the wild switch cane with Voudou men
and drummed or chanted prayers to Papa Legba.
I tried to learn to shape-shift, mixing roots
with buzzard beaks, graveyard dirt, and wood
from an oak struck leprous with zigzag lightning.
It never worked but Old Man Fullilove,
swear to God, made a deck of playing cards
scatter out of his hands like butterflies
and light on walls, a homemade mobile, and me.
Crawdead taught me the mind within the mind.
Some of the Voudou shacks had cool dirt floors.
My feet loved them and my soul loved the men,
their quiet faces, lamp-lit, sad with history—
those onyx eyes, those cotton crops of hair.

4

(*Under a chinaberry tree in Cotton Plant, Arkansas. Ancel Fullilove and I
sit on upturned buckets and share a bottle of malt liquor.*)

Mr. Fullilove: You hear Crawdead telling 'bout what happened to him down there at Ash Grove Cemetery?

Me: Naw. What happened?

Mr. Fullilove: Crawdead stay right by the graveyard now, you know.

Me: Yeah, his mama told me he moved out there.

Mr. Fullilove: Well, he say he out there in the graveyard one night and heard somebody say, "I better not catch you out here no more." He thought it was some woman flirting. She had a high, soft voice. Said, "Come here, big boy."

Ole Crawdead got happy then. He thought he finna luck out and get him some strange.

Me: Ha! That's Crawdead for you.

Mr. Fullilove: Yep, always after the pussy. So he say, "Where you at?" High, soft voice say, "Over here."

He got a little closer and seen it was a black panna with a big ole bushy tail.

mystical animal: panther

Me: Do what now? The panther was talking?

Mr. Fullilove: Yep. He told her, say, "I tell you what: I'm on go home right quick, but I'll be back directly."

That panna look at him, say, "HAYell naw! You finna go get a gun!"

And Crawdead say, "I don't know how she knowed it neither, but that sho what I finna do!"

Now when Crawdead tell that, he don't laugh, he don't smile.

5

Welcome back to Word Aflame Ministries, the most anointed, Spirit-led show on Christian talk radio. I'm your host, Terry Tightwater, and we're talking to Jim Sprig, who has a new product your church needs to know about. Tell us about your incredible new invention, Jim.

Well, Terry, I call it The Ultimate Hymnal. It's basically a computer you mount on a pulpit, and it's got over three thousand songs loaded on it.

Wonderful. So how does The Ultimate Hymnal work?

The singer just toggles through the titles, reaches out a finger, and taps the one they want. The song will start playing immediately.

Wowzers! Now that's what I call amazing.

Tell me the truth, Terry: how many times have you sat in a church service waiting on a singer to start singing, and there's some sort of technical problem that results in fifteen to twenty seconds of awkward silence?

More times than I care to remember, Jim.

You know, Terry, it might not sound like a lot, but you give the Devil fifteen or twenty seconds of silence and he can wreak all-out havoc on a church service.

Absotively posilutely! You gotta keep that thing moving. So Jim, how can our listeners find out more about installing this revolutionary new system in their very own churches?

I'm glad you asked, Terry. It's as easy as going to dubya dubya dubya ultimate hymnal dot com or calling 1-800-G-E-T-H-Y-M-N. That's 1-800-Get Hymn.

6

Crawdead:

We always called that house The Castle
where the Voudou woman stayed.
'Long about fifteen year ago
I went there with my friendboy Wade.
He knowed she did Voudou, I didn't.
We's clowning and my noggin scuffed
the ceiling fan. He scooped my hair
off the blade, afraid it was enough
for the mojo queen to hex me with.

The Castle—I seen this myself—
it would blush colors overnight.
It'd be sky-blue, yellow, or pink
one night and pea-green, say, by sunup.
Folks mighty strange, but I don't think
nobody paint they house at night.

That woman's poodle was a fright.
Thing stayed out in the road all time
and never got hit. Always hassle
pedestrians. One night, when Wade
come walking home, he pass The Castle
and that dog stands on its hind legs
like a man. All at once, it nightmares
into a monster with a bat face,
a pouch of possums, and deer antlers.

mythical dog

7

(Blues band sitting around in the practice space.)

Trent (sorting weed on a phone book): You got the Chinese chewing gum?

(Eric passes him some Zig-Zag rolling papers.)

Trent: One of these days, we're fixing to smoke you out, Greg.

Me: Maybe so.

Trent: You're missing out's all I got to say.

Eric: What's the funnest thing you ever did high, Trent?

Trent: Barged in on a Holy Roller church service. I shit you not: folks were flying around the room like birds. I stood there for about two minutes staring like a treeful of owls. I was freaked out for days.

Eric: Go to hell. I grew up in a Holy Roller church. You're the lyingest son of a bitch I ever seen.

Trent: You don't have to believe it, but it's true.

Eric: Sounds like 'shrooms to me.

Me: How high were they flying?

8

Lord, make me a flying squirrel
or a flying Holy Roller.
No, if I'm going to fly, make me a painted bunting, Lord.
Make me Sister Lou's grackle cackle and hair weirdly beautiful.
Lord, make me a fat pocketbook pearly in the St. Francis River
or an alligator gar in the Cache, Lord, and name me Black Blade.
Come on, I dare you, make me an Ozark hellbender.
Make me the fragrance of a witch hazel blooming in gelid January
or a sunset changing colors like a bruise half-healed
while a man staggers out of the rain
like a ghost through prison bars.
Lord, there's a bunch of things I want to be.
The other day I found a pad I scribbled in when I was ten or twelve.
One page said, "Greg Alan Brownderville is a boy who is,"
and then it listed words I loved.
So, Lord, all these years later, I beseech you,
make me a boy who is coal, swiss, cream, spearmint,
product, capitol, bar, marl,
quo, tap, bot, doll, roll, mat, solicitous, ma'am,
pie, toy, mellifluous, immitigable, Lord.
Make me the Choctaw hunters on the Alabama River, eating maize
granted by Unknown Woman, daughter of the Great Spirit.
Turn me into a spearmint done by top-notch scientists.
Make me a dastardly bastardly son of a bitch, Lord,
or, better yet, a rainbow roll at the sushi bar.
Make me the nutmeat patterning inside a scaly-bark hickory nut
resembling a white oak leaf or cartoon Holy Roller hands
or cartoon moose antlers, pick your image,

and feed me to rambunctious boys in the woods.
Make me a shoulder pad popping out of a football player's jersey,
flapping like a wounded wing when he's hit.
Make me the sound of Mama Windexing the tabletop—like a dog whimpering.
Make me a team of sun dogs
and a mojo in Crawdead's pocket.
Lord, I want to play Papa Legba opening the gates.
I want to see what it's like
to be a pouch of possums, dear Lord, Lion of the Tribe of Judah.
Make me a swallow of Dr Pepper in a sexy woman's mouth.
Lord, I beg of you, make me a cell phone tower a little girl dreams the Eiffel.
I want to be a wolf, Lord, or a sentence
uttered by a beautiful student from the Czech Republic:
"Greg, you never seen girl more messy like me."
Make me a swirl of actual Chinese chewing gum
hard on a pew's underside in a church meeting illegally.
Convert the gum that is me to a nipple in the lustful mind bed of a boy
after a preacher describes Bathsheba's famous rooftop bath
a little better than a boy can stand.
Make me Sister Lou's voice becoming Bathsheba's
in the imagination.
The magic nation.
I'll be David sinning and singing tragically.
Make me the silence the Devil's wreaking havoc in,
and the havoc. If you please, Lord,
make me a sheep.

past + present fsion

LAST SONG FOR BROTHER LANGSTON

That rainy day in August, I skipped work,
strung up my battered box guitar, and made
the long drive into the Ozark Mountains.
Since he had left our little church
and gone home to the hills for good,
I'd lived in fear that he would ring
my doorbell any day and sense the difference
in my life, as though he stood at Samson's door
and smelled Delilah's perfume in the air.
He would not find, I could not be, the kid
with the sandpaper voice who showed up
every Sunday to help sing down the glory.

It hurt to see him laid so low, this man
who built our church from scratch at sixty-five
and cast out devils like a nightclub bouncer.
Eyes dull as marbles, tongue tripping
over the simplest words, he mustered four:
"Brother Greg, let's sing."
I felt my way to Pumpkin Bend,
and carried all I own, my doubts, my debts,
into the music, those old songs about heaven
and being tired, about us more than God . . .
Down here the burden's heavy
and the road so rough and long
till sometimes my feet gets wearied and so sore . . .

I sing this song tonight without my partner. Jesus, let it last,
let it laugh at the moon scythe harvesting our souls:
one in the eye for death, one in the teeth of time.

II

THE WILD YONDER BLUES

FROM A NATIONALLY TELEVISED PRESS CONFERENCE
STARRING THE POETIC SHERIFF, JOSEPH KILPATRICK
CONWAY, AFTER A VAN GOGH PAINTING IS STOLEN
FROM A LITTLE ROCK EXHIBIT AND RECOVERED IN
MONROE COUNTY

interesting form

Sheriff, Sheriff Conway, Sheriff! Sheriff, we understand there was a physical struggle to apprehend Mr. Dobbs.

Yessir. It was like passionate coitus as we rolled and moaned in the dewy green of the grass, biting, scratching, tangling, while the moon sat silent on the table of the sky like a cold, stale biscuit.

Sheriff Conway, how did you locate Dobbs?

I stopped Dobbs on Highway 49, my car glittering blue in the sultry Southern night. I approached his vermilion Pontiac and he stepped out handsomely, starlight dancing on his roach of hair, a mosquito flirting with the pink swirl of his ear. All at once, he ran. I gave pursuit and wrangled him gamely to the grass near the edge of the woods.

Are there are any other suspects?

I'm not at liberty to sing of such a matter. I will say that the suspect's ears were possessed of a strange mollusklike quality like open clamshells with clams still in them. I might even say that all human ears are unspeakably strange to me in this way.

Sheriff, Sheriff! Was the painting in Dobbs's car?

Yes, ma'am, the masterpiece lay secure in the passenger seat. In the backseat a white blanket was gathered in a cumulous bundle, suggesting the cloud of hopelessness that hangs over many Third World countries today.

Where is the painting now?

The authorities here are holding the painting for now. Even as we speak, it is at a safe, undisclosed location, being watched over by my deputy Tommy Wompler, his mustache like a soft brown fuzzy worm sleeping on his lip.

ALL OF THIS ONLY FIFTY MILES FROM THE FORMER HOME OF L. FRANK BAUM, CREATOR OF *THE WONDERFUL WIZARD OF OZ*

July 1, 1955; Edmunds County, South Dakota

Bright blues and greens, the sun a faceless coin. Nine-year-old Sharon Weron, her mother trailing in a car, was riding home a freshly purchased gray-and-white mare. Sudden clouds bombed hail. The mother stopped and put a puffy black coat on the girl and said, "Cut across the field to the house. I'll take the road around and meet you." Seconds later, there it was in a camouflage sky: a clay pot on an unmanned potter's wheel. The horse fled, muscling up a high hill. The mother made it home and ran toward her daughter, whose long yellow hair swirled unmeaningfully in the wind, a drop of food coloring in a glass of water. Still astraddle the horse, Sharon ascended from the earth. She rode a thousand feet inside a whirl one witness called "a bale of wire in air." Riderless, the mare alighted in a canter. The girl landed like an airplane, let down easy into wheat the wind italicized.

Sharon tells this story with a poet's flair, but, asked what it was like to ride inside the gust, she can muster not a solitary sentence of description. Forever the best of all saying, whatever else it means, means there's something unsayable here.

This white-dust road is in for an evil storm today.
The wind seems up to something by the casual way
it whistles by. Look, sixteen miles from anywhere,
a weedy mailbox mounted on an auger,
tornadic blade ripped from a combine harvester.
This hard twist of American DNA,
Asclepian-like, has cured a teenage boy's addiction
to knocking down the mailbox in his black S-10.
The flag is a red ear against the head's bright white,
the open door a hound dog's tongue hung out,
and the letters of a letter crawl to life and bite,
black-widowing the hand that reaches in.

stray from personal

THE PALM TREE SOLILOQUIES

mythical

1. Oil Palm as Living God

The mystery men of south Benin attest:
the future is a house with sixteen doors,
and I am Fa, the sacred palm tree, blessed
with sixteen eyes to light the corridors.

2. Vai Palm as Living Man

My leafy stems are like green arrows
bringing bliss.
My leafy stems are like green arrows
bringing pain.
My lover is the rain.
Where has she gone?
I stand beside the sea alone,
shot up with eros, and cursed with this
eternal spring, living from kiss to kiss.

3. Dying Palmetto as God and Man

A thousand times you ambled down the street
with nothing but a meeting on your mind.
Surely, I thought, one day you'd notice, doubt
your eyes until your soul swore you had found

a god forsaken. Yet I wait, unseen
by scores of stumbling, beach-brown revelers.

I wait, a shaggy-headed freak, my skin
coarser than any lower animal's.

This truth escaped you, for you lacked the eyes:
With god and nature, as with man and woman,
if you extinguish one, the other dies—
as one fades, so the other in proportion.

Each time you passed my fabled multitude
of arms, these latticed limbs Arjuna viewed,
my palms were cupped and begging, reaching out.
I was hungry and you fed me not.

Paul said the flesh makes war against the spirit.
Whose flesh? I bristle every time I hear it.
Paul drank the blood and ate the holy food.
Lord Krishna played his flute in a holy wood,
luring the cowgirls from their chilly pillows,
and danced all night among the bird-glad willows.
In the Deep South I shared a pew with folks
who thought a good, full-throated prayer unchokes
the source at some invisible Siloam.
They found that flesh is worth the praying through.

I had this dream last night (may it come true) . . .
At dawn, deep in a forest far from Rome,
a blind man laid his hands on *Saint Teresa
in Ecstasy.* As he felt her marble face,
she warmed and softened. He kissed her into color—
their mingled breath burning with lovers' pleasure
and sweet with silent, grateful words of praise.
As if sheet lightning blessed his night-cursed eyes
then held its awesome flash, sight flickered twice
and he was healed. Imagine, paradise
awaiting: all that brightening beauty—day!
Still, he closed his eyes to kiss and pray.

VANILLA HOME RUN

Left arm stretching for the catch,
the difference between winning and losing,
son among the diamonds
of a mesh-metal wall
holds the perfect scoop
against a huge and hungry silence.
Woozy with heat
and the pungency of deet,
keeping self enough—just enough—
to play at having none,
he decides.
What was aimed at the black panther street's
dark mouth and green-light eyes
must not be stolen from the air,
must be "going, going, gone!"
But: for one quick tick
it's his to love—
he's there
with vanilla home run
in a sugar-cone glove.

For two months in these mountains, not a thought
of all the pleasure your lithe body might have brought
me, oh your bright, wet body, smooth and firm
but giving, giving—moonless midnight caught
in your humid eyes. For two months, with a swarm
of hornets in my head, a private storm,

I did not pluck a leaf of sycamore
and touch it to my face, nor linger to adore
a rosebush or the garden of stars in bloom.
My soul felt like a panicked prisoner
who hallucinates the shrinking of her room.
Infinite night contracted to a tomb.

But then you brushed a leaf of sycamore
across my softening face, my chest, my inner thighs.
Whispered, "You have me." Men, gods, vows of war—
forgotten when I searched your secret eyes.
My life was locked inside my bones no more.
I breathed it into you and to the skies.

Night spreads like a burn; I don't have long.
Yahweh would crush this country should I disobey.
Tell the poets I'll have no mourning song.
What are humans given but a day,
marred by fear, pain, our rage at being wronged—
one darkening day to love ourselves away?

(A playlet. Setting: a small, dark bedroom. Stormy music starts as the curtain opens. Kneeling beside his bed, a father sobs and prays for his daughter. His wife walks in and speaks, almost sings, sometimes looking out the window at her dancing daughter and imitating her movements.)

She dances on the shore of a cornfield,
wind in the muleta of her gown.
A god, a ghost? Has she been born, been killed,
and what has she to do with anyone?
A twister hisses in the warm, green skies
and flicks its tongue of lightning in the air,
stirring a rider's hunger in her thighs,
loosening pieties braided in her hair.
Don't pray. Not even Jesus can restrain
her now with puppet strings of windy rain.
Each iris like a disk of lime, her eyes
welcome the storm. Her yearnings are no wife's,
no daughter's. Father, you forget. Her life's
the answer to our own wild bodies' prayer.

SEX AND PENTECOST

Below a rind of moon in the blue soon,
the lovely, doomed light
of nearly-night,
my neighbor trespassed in my garden.

She kissed a wet tomato
and her finger curled *come.*
In her long white gown
she looked like a tornado.

For her and the spice of tomato stem
scenting the wind, for sin
and summer's green flames,
for wild lemons and pennons of the canebrake, I came.

She shed her clothes and banished mine.
Along that overdue New Mádrid line,
we fell across a strawberry bed.
I bowed my head and I kissed her where she said.

My tongue moved and she was music,
first a violence of silence and then a splash—
wet soprano, wet red soprano:
strawberry wine overbrimming a trembling glass.

I was made of pelotons,
and they were singing all at once.
I heard the noise of many waters,
learned this much of time and song:

Before there were Tongues, there was a tongue,
lungs, and loins;
and nothing matters till it matters
to sinning sons and dying daughters.

A man stumbles out of a pub in The Mumbles,
the sun a lemony anonymity in chill blue air.
Lady with button of honey hair pushes a pram, damn:
her lips, her nips, her hips, and fingertips.
She nibbles lemon creams and raspberry whips.
White slacks in stride, drawing swarms of fantasies,
evoke confederate jasmine petals, and he sees,
he smells her dare, silently implied:
"Zoom to your doom. I total any man I ride."

Then an anemone of memory, a pyrotechnic bloom . . .

He is twelve years old again, the boy blue,
woman whipping him to welts, down by the docks,
and all along the mountainsides of autumn,
treetops in rows like those of a crayon box.
"Burrow with your tongue, burrow," she instructs.
Christ my holy solar Christ
"You pray to me from here on out. I stuff and mount your gods."
I'm a stranger I'm in danger
Jesus meet me in the manger
"Shoosh. Make your mouth useful. Here's a pacifier toe."
Boy lies, flies, dies hearing, feeling her helicopter breathing.

A child, with his face mashed low,
bright wet from the buttonbush, mumbles, *Don't*
Make me—Please—Make me—Don't—
and he thinks, not in words but in the blood's vernacular:
O moon my octopus with your lightning whips tentacular am I
I may be liking this

LITTLE LOTTY KNOX

Necklaced for breakfast,
she is served her daddy's eardrums—
little Lotty, little Lotty Knox.
No emotion wreaks commotion
in her eyes of frozen ocean
as she dissertates on Keats,
and her whorled platinum locks
are like cha-ching machine receipts.

When sugarplum comes in a 'Vette
(toe polish red because she said),
the daughter show must end.
Her Exquisiteness declares,
"I'm going out to walk the boyfriend."

Invisible reins, invisible reins.
Coca-Cola, Coca-Cola fizzing in her veins.

Upstairs, the elders say their prayers,
hoping she'll be better
than to let her gentleman caller, she so young,
leave her a shoddier body or even taste her tongue.
Crazywhile, she toys with boy-oh-boy,
plays oscillating kiss-heads by the jacaranda,
as her tiny, shiny puppies
are beeping about the grand veranda.

Star of the world parade,
the honey boss, the magic maid,
Miss Lotty flicks attention, piddling glints,
at all the plebs and debs and gents.

Every bootblack, every hoe hand,
every woman and man of leisure
craves a wafer of her pleasure.

When she's gone, her glimmery memory
hovers doveless above her lovers,
who quote their 1 Corinthians
against the Cyprian,
who say, "Love wins as it loses.
It's the beautiful saviour the world abuses."

When she's here, they neither see her
as a sacrificial mirror
nor fear that they control her,
that she lives to let their myriad dreams ensoul her.
There's no time. When Lotty Knox
ascends to her sunroof seat
and floats down any street,
love pounces on the pavement—
love, it scrabbles among the rocks,
and it fights and bites the children
for a glittering, skittering sweet.

PANJANDRUM

Having left his quean Savannah
at the piano
stoking Prokofiev,
the moon seemed a breve
above Panjandrum, as he tripped
on his whiskey through a city gone dead
and fed to the forest.
Streets like these, he thought,
ought to be bought
by the Game and Fish.
He twisted his ankles
among the honeysuckle strangles.
Beware the trees, beware.
Let them, trees will net you in the shadows of their branches.
Stars crawled, crawled all over the air,
got in his hair,
and spun him a gossamer galaxy.

Meantime, his red-tressed autoantonym
undressed in the glum
among the high drapes and pie safes
of the deteriorarium.
His fathers had calloused their hands'
hands indoorsing woman;
fidgeted when a man made of night
gripped a child-bearing baluster
and screwed it into place.
Now the white peeled off in scales.
Round here his family told the tales,

but the jungle slithered in from the fen
and tangled the town green.
He worried about his quean.

Then this evening happened,
all he'd feared.
Panthers tantrummed
and ran the Panjandrum
through a sticker-wicked thicket
and back to the damned mansion.
They disappeared,
the shadowcats, and left him panting
on his hackly, boot-bent doorstep.

Savannah, sipping wine
she'd made with rosehips,
quit the fainting couch
and strutted from the house,
on through the columns.
All calabash curves and cowrie-shell lips,
the queen was bare except for shoes and earrings.
He bowed at her red heels
to kiss their chili pepper toe tips.
Her cameo clip-ons
pinching
like lady-making language parasitic on her ears,
she took them off
and put them on her mad, star-bitten man.
"No son—I'm done,"
she said, and with a laugh,
away she went, a tipsy gypsy.
All the world's and no one's.

Then the lynching.
Panjandrum climbed a black gum on his lawn

and hung himself like jewelry—
swung alone where the jungle trespassed,
dangling participially.

CONFESSION

I have never been in love.
But remember when you
did the downward dog on my floor,
laughing, your balance off,
thanks to my homemade limoncello?
You stayed the night
and left before I woke.
Your fragrance on the pillow,
verbena, sweat, and smoke,
I wondered if I might.

more mature
love — no longer a child

1

My grandma painted pictures of her face
on junkyard treasures—lightbulbs, globes, ball bearings.
My favorite was a frowning yellow vase
with messy eyes like boot-squashed blueberries.
Two years after she died, we bought a house
along a fault line. I remember fearing
the vast black fields would crack as bright as lightning,
hell's glow exposed. Though far from marvelous,
our first tremor caused Grandma's vase to dance
off my dresser and break across the floor.
I sat up half the night, my smooth, small hands
roughened with glue, puzzling shards back together.
The years have hidden that pale vase. I fear
it may be lost, lost the crevices
like fault lines on the face, mapping her spirit.
By now I can't be sure: did she paint those,
or were they cracks I mended carefully?
There is no one to ask. No one knows.
Everything that shatters is a mystery.

2

Sam Doyle, an artist of the Gullah Islands,
painted in the colors of coastal moons
and with a virtuosic violence—
high art in Voudou vision, blues cartoons.
I motored into Sam Doyle country once
and found a gallery with two or three

of those wild works he used to trade for whiskey.
A docent told me Doyle believed the haints
he often painted fled their sweetgrass jungle
when a car first disturbed the island night.
Most of his art would leave the coast, as well.
Picking strawberry guava, a man outside
the gallery said he remembered Doyle.
He called him Uncle Sam and I thought, *Yes,*
but one we never knew. Breathing the smell
of a salt wind rattling the wild palmettos,
I wondered where a car-shy haint might flee,
now that birds nest in Walmarts' *R*'s and *A*'s.
Everything that scatters is a mystery.

3

A scientist says to me, "I thrive on knowing."
For twenty years he's researched one scant slice
of brain. I get it. Granddaddy's been hoeing
one garden plot for even longer. It's nice
to know a passage of the world by heart.
From om to amen, sacred books agree,
the world is words. One myth says destiny
is cosmic mail, epistolary art.
Science, then, is grammar. And power to it,
that noble, necessary enterprise!
Praise be for ophthalmology and yet
it can't tell all that's in a lover's eyes.
The world poem, if parsed, will not reveal
its meanings one and all and settle matters.
What we know, we never know in full,
for all around our best interpreters,
vases are dancing, spirits flying free.
Everything that shatters, everything that scatters,
everything that matters is a mystery.

III

BECOMING HOT TAMALE CHARLIE

Got a habanero heart and it ain't no wonder.
Raised in the habanero heat of Delta summer.
I's born in '21 on Sunnyside Plantation.
Grandpa drug the family here in 1899.
The mayor of Rome, Prince Ruspoli,
said Arkansas a land of many plenty. "Here, sign
the planter's contract. It's okay you can't read English."

He told Italian peasants the cotton was endless,
and shimmer like sun stunning on the blue.
"Sunnyside," ha! Mighty pretty picture what he drew.
She fertile, that much true, ten thousand acre
of the best damn cotton country mixed up by the Maker.
With Memphis upriver and New Orleans down south,
she good for crop and shipping, ain't a lick a doubt.

But Sunnyside a crooked country all her own,
a twenty-mile smug smile of ground,
lipped off by the banks
of the Mississippi and a great big lake,
except for a crack at the southeast corner,
but even in the midnight black,
toothy goons with guns bite down on the border.

The prince never bother telling my grandfather
how the planter own your soul 'fore you ever cross the water,
else Grandpa never would a left the Marche.
In debt in the Delta, dago can't flee the farm. Who say?
Law say! Even if the reason he leaving
be to earn some pay—unsnap the trap of sharecrop debt—
while his family stay behind to keep the cotton on track.

Gnaw gnaw, prince never mention that,
or how you work barefoot
and hungry sun to sun, slaving
when it's too hot to see,
then spend all fall scrapping every last lock.
He never spoke of sultry summer Europe can't match,
hotter'n two mice fucking in a wool sock.

Never told how every face at Sunnyside,
codger to the youngin, turn clear as a onion,
then yellow, then green as the stinking drinking water
from the swamp. Or how every glassy eye squint for a future
through a fever, mosquitoes fogging by the millions
like a shadow-black halo, biting piles of Italians
to the dark dirt forever. Never.

Hog-killing day, wind face-chap cold.
   Fever got me good, woozing up my thought.
   I seeing triple, hunger fangs take a hold.

Fire over water in a big black pot,
   Papa slit hog throat, rope him round the head,
   hang him from a gum tree, douse him right hot,

shave him cleany pink. Next part I dread.
   Stab hog in the heart, let bright blood.
   For blood pie sake, save a pail a red.

Rain, sleet, snow blows up, make shitty mud.
   Stray mutt twitchy from the swamp, slobber beard,
   coughing like a brimstone preacher 'mongst the crud.

One dog, see, make three to me. I get skeered.
   Papa toss him hog-gut slime. Sky's dark guts
   ooze out, turn the light blue-weird.

Papa clean intestines and, checking for cuts,
   blow them up a like balloons. Mash B-grade meat
   for sausage links and the salt-skin gobbets

dry to cracklin's. Tongue, lips, ears, and feet
   pickled or ground to hog's head cheese.
   Ain't too much here a man can't eat.

Loin for *lonza,* quarters for *prosciutto.* Sugar, yeast,
   meal, and raisin make cake out of boiled backbone.
   Drop liver, heart, and kidney fresh in a grease,

sizzle with some pepper, salt, and onion.
   Scramble brains with eggs and fry.
   Cut fat and skin in bits, boil them in a cauldron

for the family lard—year supply.
   Muddy man-shadows, making rag soap, scald
   waste fat and mix it up with lye.

Only hair, hoof, intestine goop, and teeth get culled.
   No smokehouse, no stable,
   so we move inside. Papa rub a thick coat a salt

in a fat slab. We store it on the cypress table
   in my leaky room, where it smells
   up my dreams. Dirty snow buries my Bible,

chills my bed. Through knotholes
   in the floor of my head, I see a red-eye rabid dog
   and I'm skeered every night when the black blanket falls,

I'll feed a snorting ghost ripped from a hog.

Come a toad strangler that day, I remember.
Kids wobble off the bus, umbrellas blooming.
Three bullies, white American, thowed rocks
at Splendi Pretti's creamy little leg.
I watch, too frayed to fight. Oh how she holler,
lord, run and dance, holding her head! Three big girl,
white American too, make them boy stop.

Same day, Miss Snodgrass take Splendi's sack lunch,
homemade garlic bread and *lonza,* set it
on the sill outside the window. Did the same
to Antonio's and Dominic's, and let
the white Americans hee-haw monstrous loud,
"Tommy Salami and Tony Baloney!
Tommy Salami and Tony Baloney!"
She pass my desk and say, "Charlie, I need
to put your lunch out, too. It has an odor."

I fire back, "Must be your lunch, Miss Snotgrass.
Mine's a poke sallet sandwich, ribbon cane,
and hickory nuts."

                    She say, "Show it to me."

I grab my sack and say, "You want to see,
I let you see all right." I tump it out
on my desk, grip the hickory nut hammer,
say, "You know, Miss Snotgrass, this girl here
goes home a-hungry nearbout every day
'cause a stray dog paw through her sack and gobble
all her good food."

I stand. Teacher snap, "Carlo!
You sit your little bottom down this second!"

But something ail me like I done gone deef
and seeing through a hazy blur a smoke.
My body burning cold, like snow-bit hands
when you run hot water over them. "No need
to fool with pushing up that window," say I,
and swing my hickory hammer through the glass.
Crack like thin ice. I flunk the seventh grade
over that stunt and mighty proud I did.

CARLO FINDS OUT WHERE HIS NEW FRIEND'S NAME CAME FROM

Made me a friend at Sunnyside,
a twenty-year-old guy named Human.
He plant some cayenne pepper seed
among the cotton 'cause the straw boss
wouldn't let us grow no garden.
On the front porch of Human's quarters,
he keep a splintery church seat
we called the pepper pew. That's where
we always roost, gobble a pail
of red-hot devil-finger peppers
like most folks chomp on grapes. One day
I ask, "How come they call you Human?"

He say, "One time at the company store,
some dude say a white girl been sneaking
off in the woods with a black boy.
The old Ku Klucker at the till
talk with a skinny goat whine, say,
'If you take a blob of mud
and a scoop a iced cream and mash them up
together, you've totally rurnt the iced cream
and hadn't done a goddamn thing
for the mud.'

            "'Bout that time, he say,
'Nigger, you need help with something?'
I stare him down. His scabby face
look like a peeling gourd. I say,
'I ain't a nigger. I'm a human.'
He spit some chew, say, 'Alright, Human.

What you need?' Everybody laugh
and I been Human ever since."
He stopped and waited. I hush hush.
"Damn, Carlo! You just gonna sit there?
This is me telling you the story,
not the shit happening again.
At least laugh. That's one way to own
it all." I laughed a little chuckle
and reached in the pail, wishing things
was different. Chawing a jaw full
of pepper, Human say, "It's good
you practicing up on eating heat.
You fixing need it round these parts."

CARLO CUTS A ROSE FOR SPLENDI PRETTI

During snow time
Human learnt me
how to wade my way
through swampland out
of Sunnyside, a secret route
where the watchmen never hide.
No cause to fret, Human say,
if mink or muskrat see.

'Long about the first a May,
when the woods had done their greening,
in the cool of the evening,
I led my Splendi Pretti
through the muddy muddy bottoms.
I was loving every heartbeat. Sometimes
when we had to cross a slough,
she rode in my rough arms.
Rode my shoulders too.
I stopped to show
her blue flag blossoms
and sweet bay. Also devil's shoestring,
prized for its magic roots.
'Long the border of the woods,
a mansion stood
with bright white columns
like big old prison bars.
That's where a fancy lady
name a Miss Willette lived like a queen
and used her honey-dripper accent
to sweet-talk her plants into staying good and green.
Me and Splendi sneak around

the arbor, made our way
through the parterres, and found
a sweet booby bush. I pulled
a blossom like a Southern lady would
of a spring Sunday morning.
Splendi let me do the honors, press
it down her dress
between her warm condolences.
She loved to wear that strawberry guava smell.
Pretty soon we come
to Splendi's favorite sight.
Miss Willette, or her yard boys,
done rooted all
the wild plants out
and grown white roses in the bare dark soil.

Which ain't too fun
in southeast Arkansas. The wet heat
give a rosebush black spot
and the dug dirt fool
the woods into thinking
nature cleared some land for them
with lightning fire, a twister, or a hurricane,
so the pioneer brush come a-brambling in:
square canes of blackberry—
with their tough, deep roots, quick to thicket—
shoot up round the roses.
And the loose, watered ground
make a rose want to spread beyond the bounds
the goddess of the garden plotted out.

Me and Splendi leaned low
to breathe the funeral-smelling flowers
we both loved. We forgot about
the fact we tapped a devil's-snuffbox in the forest,

getting smoky chocolate dust
on our cotton-picking fingers,
which smudged the soft white petals.
Trying to work around the stickers,
I cut a rose for Splendi
and watched her brown eyes flicker
like puddles do in rain.
I like how the late sun
honeyed up her skin
as I wrapped the rose
in pawpaw leaves
I'd picked off on the way,
took her hand, and laid some beauty in it.

For the better part of a minute,
I stood there looking at her,
wondering if anything could ever
be so beautiful again,
and nowaday, when I think it over,
I think she might have been
all the prettier, all the holier
for the soul-grinding, man-bleeding,
mansion-raising order
that tagged our people dagos, tried us,
kept us deep in prayer
with black dirt on our hands and face,
dying early all too often,
but with laughter in our coughing.

I had a blurry-border-thought
that what I felt with Splendi was
the magic both, the magic in-between—
suffery brambles moving in
and the white rose of coldness moving out.
She was the only bloom I cared about.

The fallen sun was playing Midas,
so I thanked the good Lord
as a red-wing blackbird
lit to shit some berry seeds beside us.

CARLO GOES TO THE NEW CATHOLIC CHURCH NEAR SUNNYSIDE

Swarmed and a-hassled by a black cloud
of mosquitoes, I pressed on, cruising for a blessing,
barged into church for the Saturday confession.
I learnt real quick-a-like, Italians ain't allowed.
Four folk waiting, lounging 'long a pew,
two mumbling penance, done gone through.
Irish lady say, "Do something, Stu.
We can't have dagos in our church."

Stu rush me like a bouncer at a jook joint door.
I stumble tumble rumble, ass first in the dirt.
Stu boom, "Don't let me catch you here no more."
I puzzled, ask why. He grumble, say, "You don't belong here, son."
I never got forgiven for the tressy-messy roll the night before.
Splendi Pretti, Splendi Pretti, look the damage what you done.

CARLO LEARNS ABOUT BETRAYAL WHEN HIS GIRLFRIEND LEAVES HIM FOR "GLITTERY EYES"

Me and Human was on the pepper pew.
He munched a pointy red heart of cayenne.
I let it rip: "Welp, Splendi threw that leg
on a rich man's son, won herself a ticket
out a Sunnyside."

                "Ah well," Human mumbled.

"She come to see me while ago," I said.
"Told me bye. Claim his eyes all 'glittery,'
said please don't hate her but she fixing marry
this cream puff, everwho he is. I try
be glad for her sake, glad she getting free,
but it's hard. Glittery eyes! Sound plumb prissy.
It kills me. Kills me, Human. Graveyard dead."

     "Shit fire, save the matches!" Human said.
"I can't listen to this. Don't act like some
mistreated lover boy. You ain't been true
to that girl one full week since y'all been calling
yourself a-going steady. And she ain't
been true to your ass neither."

                    "You a lie!"

"Think again," Human said. "Honey, you crazy
as a bessybug if you don't think she knowed
your ways or never got in on the game.
Hell, man, I diddled her a coupla times
madamnself. How you like them apples, playboy?"

68

CARLO SPEAKS OF HOT TAMALES

Human learnt me how to make them.
I's over to his place one day
when he was doing up a batch.
Told me, say,
"Christmas coming fast,
and I got peoples bussing in
from off. You know what that mean.
Time to cook. My city kin
don't cut a fool no slack.
One year they whup the devil out of poor old Human
with these hot tamales. Had to make
a heaping bunch for folks to carry back."

Down through the years
Human use coon, quail, goat, deer,
possum, blackbird-rabbit mix, and squirrel,
but his trusty standby was pork shoulder.
We put one in a pot with water,
spice it with red pepper,
garlic, salt, and onion,
boil her till she done,
and grind her out. We save the broth
and mix it with some meal to make a masa,
let it set overnight
so the flavors get to know each other nice and slow.
Human say, "First thing, when you bite
into a tamale, you fixing taste the dough,
so you gotsta make it hot. I make mines red."
And boy did he ever.
Human say Odell, his second cousin,
a street-corner hot tamale peddler,

had a saying: *Red dough make the green dough.*
He raked in twenty cent a dozen.

Odell and Human learnt about tamale
from Jesus, a Mexican gandy dancer,
one year scrapping cotton in McGehee.
Every day, come lunchtime, Odell and Human unpack
a hunk of cornbread, so much colder and blander
than their friend's tamales, still warm in the sack.
Tamales give a person energy—
good to boost a
hoe hand, wo' slap out by noon.
Jesus would make the others wild with envy
when he moan and moan
and nod and whisper, "Exquisitos, a mi gusto."
Jesus explained the recipe
and say he learn it down in Mexico from a Indian.
Odell tweaked it, made it his own.
Human couldn't call to mind exactly which ingredients
were added, but he say they made a difference,
made tamale taste black.

Folks used to wrap with corn shuck,
but lazy crazies in the twenty-first century
gone to parchment paper. Old way's better.
When it's all scrolled together,
that corn flavor count. Parchment paper
got a wax to it. When you cook,
wax get in your hot tamale,
you gone taste that little bit of yuck.
Hot tamale gotta be so yum,
you want to suck the shuck.

Once the dough get red and ready,
spread it on your wrap and fork some meat
off on it. Then roll them

and tie them. Nice and neat.
Ain't no sauce left, whip some up,
'cause, man, you drench them babies,
they right tasty: folks'll eat
the fool out of them tamales,
little red firecrackers, packed with heat.
Speaking of crackers: saltines make
the last tick on your fixings checklist.
Milk optional. Some folks take
milk with tamale for their breakfast.

Human say his cousin's motto go like this:
Make the dough, make the filling,
roll it up, and make a killing.
Say he had a honey of a business.
Human use to help him bark
on Cherry Street in Helena from dusk on into dark,
and said the smell got so delicious,
folks was bumping into parking meters,
staring, wondering what that heaven was,
spicing up their neighborhood.
Them hot tamale mama-slapping, shuck-licking good.

They say it all started with the Indians.
It don't make a spit in the river's worth a difference.
Human say,
"Indians, Mexicans, blacks, whites, and now Eye-talians,
we all equal in love of tamale." Nowaday,
rich planter man go to fancy, five-star restaurant
to nibble hot tamale. He don't want
to face the maker, some greasy-fingered papa,
but we all mixed up, brother, mixed up in that masa.

Got tired of smelling mule farts all damn day, every day,
so I decided to become a colored man. Late one night,
I pack my ragbag, steal away from Sunnyside,
and walk to the hills. I kindly look and talk black anyway.

Went to a junkyard, found me a mower and some boards,
built a box, mount it on the wheels and axles of the mower,
paint it white, and hung a coal-oil lantern on the bar
so I could see and be seen. I paint red words

on the front and sides: HOME-STYLE HOT TAMALES!
40¢ A DOZEN! SHUCK-LICKIN' GOOD!
I found some colored farmers, strutted cocky as I could
to their door, said, "Howdy, folks, I'm Hot Tamale Charlie!

I'm new in Beulah, a street-food peddler and a Voudou man.
Geddy, god of the underground, tells me money buried
on y'all's land, Confederate treasure. I'm alone, ain't married
nor a daddy. You folks let me live here a little span

and cook in your kitchen, I'll buy all my own groceries
and use my powers to witch for money. If I find it,
I get half and you get half." I flashed a contract and they signed it.
Should have got out years ago, I done it with such ease.

"Hot Tamale Charlie here!
Get your hot tamales!"
I yelled it over and over
that Friday night on the main drag
in Wilmot, Arkansas. A chilly breeze
blew up, turned to a snowy gust,
and made them tail a Spanish moss
flop and wag
like a grinnel in the dust.
I wore my old quilt-looking overalls,
patched up blue and orange,
red and yellow. Suddenly I felt a heart twinge.
It was Splendi Pretti,
little bitty beauty
in a pink dress, hair all done up
in a black button.
I hadn't thought to see that girl again,
but there she was, switching up the street.
She smiled, come to a stop.

"Hot Tamale Charlie!" she said.
"I'm starving. Give me half a dozen."
But her friendgirl said, "I wouldn't."
Splendi quizzed her as to why.
"I heard my Uncle Tillman say
niggers make those nasty things with cat meat,"
the girl replied.
Splendi looked me dead in the eye
a coupla seconds, then turned away.
And all the little snows,

strange in the streetlight
like albino mosquitoes,
flurried round my straw hat,
flying in my eyes. I squinted,
watching my Splendi walk off past the bright,
jingly stores, slip into a small red car,
and disappear in the white distance.
So mine not long ago, I thought,
so mine, she gone as gone can be,
another fellow's missus.
That was 1943,
two days to Christmas.

HOT TAMALE CHARLIE SINGS OF A PLAYER'S HEARTBREAK

I courted bad girls and never thought twice.
"I love the lies in their eyes,"
I told the boys. "I want to try the venom in 'em.
Give me lawless women.
If they kill me, that's all right. Everybody dies.
And hell gets all the bad girls clear from Arkansas to Yemen."
That's what I believed, and I sho God paid the price.

If you meet a chilly honey with her friends collecting dew
and everybody's laughing by the time the night is through,
chances are, the joke's on you.
She'll let you make runs in her black thigh-highs
like a airplane leaves in dusky skies.
Go ahead and crash.
Crash tonight at her place.
Let your dreams buzz around in the perfume of her airspace.
There's bound to come a morning, when you turn to kiss her face,
you'll be doing good to find a stray black eyelash
on the pillowcase.

It was a still, chill morning, sky was clear—
the first cold snap of a warm, wet fall.
Walking back to Beulah from a all-night blues dance
in Seven Devils Swamp, where I sold hot tamales
to the good-timing people,
I come upon a pasture full a wild oregano.

I seen the white puffs all over the ground
like somebody dropped a bunch of Kleenex,
or windblown slips of paper.
Must have been a hundred fifty,
some five inch long.
The sap of wild oregano freezes, bulges,
splits the stems lengthwise,
then flows a-loose, whitening when it touches air.
As more sap comes,
ice taffies out
like fingernails angling for the Guinness World Record
in swirling loops, cones, fancy curls,
bouquets, or lacy ribbons—
unlifely blooms slitting green throats.

Some people calls it rabbit ice
'cause it looks like a passel
of cottontails white in the weeds.
I done heard a bunch of names:
frost flowers, ice blossoms,
frost angels, feather frost, ice castles.

When ice oozes out of the pores in wood,
I call it whitebeards,

'cause one time rabbit hunting,
me and Human seen ice on a dark dead branch
propped against a tree.
Human say it look like hair,
make him think about old Santy Claus
or the Heavenly Father
and I say, "Yeah, or Brer Rabbit
stuck everwhichaway to the Tar-Baby."

That morning I come home from Seven Devils,
one piece a rabbit ice
look like the floor-sweeping, hooped white
satin skirt of a chilly Southern belle.
I knelt down to see it up close,
and had a vision I been wrestling ever since . . .
Under that skirt is the body of beauty
that smothers this Africa-beaked bluebird head of a globe.
When the planet cracks, Belle gone smile
on lily high and say, "It's hatching."
And all the thoughts in our imagination
gone spill like brain yolk, then grow feathers and flit free
like bluebird memories, free in a sky the same color as they are.
All sex, no motherhood, Belle gone tower up among them,
and she'll be awful beautiful a minute.
But Belle, the bluebirds, and the sky will all go silver,
then the words. Ain't no name for pleasure
when it's all there is and no one's there to feel it.

So what about the being and the doing,
the hoping and the hurting?
What did all the dying mean?

One piece of ice close to the hoopskirt
was a strange scroll I couldn't read—
sparkle-blind white,

all them word-glitter dancing with the daylight,
dancing clean out of their selves.

The sun had the last word,
said noon would never see that magic parchment,
that cold tamale eaten by the air.

IV

GHOSTS

ARKANSAS BLACKS

The boy's first night there, he took a flashlight
down stairs worn smooth by his grandfathers' boots.
He raised the latch, opened the heavy door
to a translucent veil of cobwebs, and guided
a cone of light slowly across the room.
From the floor joists that formed the cellar ceiling,
dozens of nails jutted out, sewing strings
looped over them and knotted to the stems
of Arkansas blacks, fruit that keeps. But time
had mummified these apples, left to hang
for twenty years or more, the boy guessed.
A few steps in, he was transformed, a ghost
in cobweb robes. He reached out, his pale fingers
touching dark apple skin. The light trembled.
How will I ever sleep in this damned house?

Sundown and the fields are burning black.
Stung lungs tighten, laughs coarsening to coughs,
but friends and kin still gather
at J.R.'s crumbledown shanty.

J.R. shreds his voice over a grate of song.
The knife he uses for a slide blurs
like cotton middles through the window of a train.
Once, by chance, his guitar's whine
matches pitch with a swinging door.

Everyone fills up on barbequed coon
and swigs from the same jug of stump-water whiskey.
A sixty-something farmhand
dances like he has a wasp up his pants leg.

Some of the boards on the hackly porch
are loose, turn into trapdoors,
but J.R. knows their snatching darkness
and how to work around them.

That laugh. Like sand caught in his throat.

Wet with sweat, snaky veins on his temples,
he attacks the black body
of his guitar with a rhythmic picking hand,
his knife against the strung-up neck.

Women hunched around a table
play Georgia skins, eyeing their cards
and cramming bills in rusted coffee cans.

GOBLIN SONG

Mudcat Myers
got a one-bottle bottle tree—
empty RC
on a knuckly branch
like a slide about to jam
on the highline wires.

Inside Mudcat's one-bulb house,
pet rats
named Racecar, Bess, and Mable
scurry over the couch and table.
Scrawled across the wall,
dead numbers haunt a dead telephone.

Jug of corn whiskey
and the party's on.

He cups a French harp,
makes it bawl
with a night-greased,
rusty-roof,
black-shack tone,
and he wails by his lonesome . . .

Got a goblin in my pocket
gobblin' money all day long.
Goblin in my pocket
gobblin' money all day long . . .

The goblin's taken everything.
Unless you count the song.

A WELDER'S NEW YEAR'S EVE

Another ice storm, someone else is dead.
She's on a ditch bank in the car she crashed.
Sixteen years old. The lone eyewitness said
she tried to round McDaniel's Curve too fast.

It's a small town, I've fixed this car before.
That time, the accident made a widower
of my old coach. And now I'll exorcise
a ghost with auburn curls and a smashed skull,
scour the bloodstains, take this twisted steel
and make it gleam again so that fresh eyes
might look on it with innocence. Perhaps
a year from now someone will buy it for
a son or daughter's sweet sixteen. One hopes.
And I'll be damned if there's a trace of her
perfume to haunt the senses when I'm done.

December's dying: 5, 4, 3, 2, 1.
A momentary welder in the weather
bears down on the cold, silver pavement, arcs,
and melts the new year and the old together—
lightning on ice, a blinding spray of sparks.

Bonding the now and then I'm paid to sever,
I live in paradox. For all my fireworks,
all my skill, the Old Acquaintance reappears.
These hands can do some good. One hopes. One fears.

TABLELAND AT ZERO

At church this morning, Sister Phada
sung a special called "Higher Ground."

Lord, lift me up and let me stand
by faith on heaven's tableland.

Ever time I hear that song,
I see a quail and manna picnic,

a potluck in the wilderness.
Sister Phada raised her hand and closed her eyes,

whining high and country
with a voice of pure banana cream Jesus.

No one had your pew.
A new boy seemed at home in mine.

Night's on its way from Georgia,
spreading white icing on the world.

Soon I'll disappear into the woods again.
Till then I'll sit and talk

and watch you whilst you sleep.
I am zero years old now, Two-Mama.

Few years back, when I was only six,
you told me, "Never make snow cream

out of the first snow of the year.
The first one purifies the air."

    That night last summer, just before
I drownded, me and Sister laid face-up

on a sandblow, my lips ajar with awe.
Looking at me from the side, she said,

"The Big Dipper's a-pourin stars
in your mouth, Brother!" So I swallowed

and they purified me like a snow. Then
I went dissolving in the river.

Anymore, I don't desire to sup or sip,
other than to swig the stars. Last week,

Cache River froze to a crystal highway,
but the water fell out, swagging planks

of ice cracking, collapsing, disappearing
into the swamp, but still, around

a thousand tupelos and cypress,
glass tabletops hold, serving nothing,

nothing: clear, clean, holiest nothing.
Don't be afraid, Two-Mama.

I know the cancer hurts right now,
but tomorrow's your zeroeth birthday.

He ties the boat to a tree that he can trust
where the wild sugarhaws of Arkansas
rain red berries after a killing frost,
rare fruits his brother Bobby helps him haul
away with crackle-wood steps. In the boat,
working his shoestrings free of cockleburs,
he breathes the bayou mud funk as they float
past cypress hips. After their mother stirs
that appley pink translucence, Bobby grins
and licks the wooden spoon, smearing his chin.
Then he holds a jar up, hot and bright,
to see its coral color in the light.
Too soon those pops, the sealing of the lids,
mutate to muffled blasts. Ten more dead. Kids.

TERROR

Heart like a bomb
strapped to your chest and ticking,
walk into the world.

A SOLDIER GETS HOME

Ending my bluebird days of boyhood, war
seduced me, war I could romanticize—
a belly dance of rippling sand and fire—
until the hot dust gusted in my eyes,
and stars, glimmers of God, became the sky's
bullet holes. Home for seven months, I've wondered
if home's a fiction only a fool buys.
The other morning, a turtle crossed my front yard.
His hut, battered and scuffed, said he could be a hundred,

and right away the image activated
a memory . . . Blizzard of butterflies, late April.
A gem-eyed boy stripping a twelve-pound flathead,
I had pulled his mudsuit bright side out to the tail
and laid him open when a dome-shaped turtle
moved in the belly. "Look, Dad! Can I have
it for a pet? Jonah the Miracle!"
My father told me Jonahs can't survive
outside the hungry swamps that swallow them alive . . .

But suddenly, in my ravaged mind, the picture
morphed and the dark-green shell became a helmet.
Crawling with nightmares, it came to claim a soldier,
some head to haunt. I tried so hard to gut
my memory. Better that its joys be cut
away than grief-diseased, harrowed and hollowed,
or so I told myself. Today at sunset,
my windows going blind, I hit the remote
and a war film was on. I cursed, but when it showed

a GI chin deep in a smoky ditch,
the TV's rounded screen bagging his helmet
like the see-through stomach lining of a fish,
a cruel metaphor went bright side out.
Imagery that had stolen Jonah brought
him back to me. Closing my eyes, the turtle
in my hands again, I knew I had to set
him free and trust him to be swallowed whole—
trust him to nest inside the darkness like a soul.

A SWISS VINTNER IN THE LAND OF MUSCADINES

Autumn, 1882: A Letter to His Brother in the Old Country

It's Sunday morning on St. Mary's Mountain,
the Ozark sunrise a wet watercolor of pink and blue,
a hawk's call the harshest sound.
Last year, I crossed the swamp
without a solitary dollar to rustle in my palm,
and now I stand on my own wine-growing ground,
a thousand feet above the valley's hardwood bottomland,
patchwork fields of sorghum cane and whitening cotton,
the silver slither of the river.

Twining through my cloud-hooded woods
are wild whiskery vines
bearing grapes called muscadines,
"musky dimes" in local speech,
some as big around as a five franc piece.
Their shiny skins black and dotted,
they're like little candied planets,
night-coated and flecked with stars.

After a punishing summer, only here and there
have I found a shriveled one,
what they call a "mummy dime."

Honeysuckle, akebia, and other floral immigrants
strangle trees, but muscadine goes easy on its host,
tendrils clinging tightly
then lightly before they rot off altogether,
fresh growth braceleting the branch further upward.

This is musky dime time,
the cool of autumn blowing in.
Ozarkers gather dimes by the basketful.
Careless of stains, boys hold their shirts out to bag them.

I found these grapes September a year ago.
When I walked into the woods, their musky smell came over me
like memory somehow mine though not yet made.
A young man and woman were laughing,
eating from a loaded vine.
Playing coy, she ran away, dashing under high trees,
her scarlet hair aflicker, muscadines squelching
under her bare white feet.
He caught her in a tumbling kiss,
their lips doubtless tingling
from the acid of the grapes.
Pure sin to watch, I know.
I must be shriven soon.
But could you have looked away
when he kissed her purple-blotched feet?

Glad boy bandits came yowling past me,
chucking dimes at one another.
One boy, a grape whirring toward his head,
made a mad leap for a muscadine rope and swung across a ravine.
They called a truce and ate themselves weary,
tongue-threshing, spitting seeds and skins.

My curious hand tendriling
the silver-smooth wood of muscadine,
I didn't think of jelly, hull pie,
candied skins, not even wine.
All asizzle with boyhood, wanting nothing but a taste,
I shuffled through the leaves and plucked a pretty one,
dropped it sun warm in my mouth.

When I bit, it gushed on my tongue
and slid loose down my throat.
I tasted all the musk and sugar of ripening night,
of a wild girl rolling through the ticklish weeds alone.
Down to skin, I tongued its inner lining
for the sweetest juice and tenderest flesh.

For muscadines, so thick and tough the hulls,
our grape dance needs emphatic feet;
it might not work at all.
We'll see. Did you catch that "we"?
Tell me something, brother.

Are you at home at home? Unfolding Europe
on my desk tonight, I tried to dream away
the distance, but looking at that wrinkled map,
varicose with rivers, I could say
"Old World." Come. I invite you with a quill
a hawk wafted my way. If you're vacillating,
hold this paper to your face and smell:
I'm using the blood of muscadines for ink.

Bugs fired and the windshield cracked: a crystal bull's-eye.
He meant to drop a grackle, a shimmering
of black and blue like superhero hair.
Picking tomatoes, Brother Abbot turned,
saw what his son had done, and moseyed over
to inspect. He loved that bright red truck, a gift
from the church for Pastor Appreciation Month.
Without a word he stepped inside the house,
and when he stormed back out cocking a rifle,
Bugs and his buddies dropped their weapons and ran.

"Come back here, boys!" he laughed. "I was just playing."
He gave his son a dutch rub, smiled, and said,
"Look here—y'all want to hunt some birds for real?
Hop in the truck." They piled into the back,
all guns and grins, Bugs bounding over the tailgate
to claim the silver toolbox as his throne.
They jostled down those Mohawked country roads
to Abbot's eighty acres of muscadines,
wreathed by a forest full of birds. The boys
leapt down, their feet poofing the hot white sand
of the turnrow. Abbot said, "You boys stay put."

Three lush green aisles away, a black man stooped,
sacking dark, bright fruits. He saw the pickup
and froze like a photograph. The preacher grumbled,
"Seems I got a coon loose in my vines."
He slammed the door and swaggered toward the man.
"What in tarnation? Cain't be Mister Midnight!
If you had witchy powers like you claim,
you would a known to stay at home today."

Shiny with sweat, the Voudou man stood silent.
"This land is posted. See that purple paint?"
Abbot moved closer. Indigo buntings chittered
like spry old ladies at the beauty parlor.
"How come you smell like spirit of turpentine?
Y'all still use that for chest rub? I'd a guessed
you got your fill of turpentine back yonder
before the camp closed down. You soaked up plenty
in your day. If I ran you through a still,
I'd prolly get a good ten-gallon yield."
Mister Midnight said nothing. "Tip your hat
and show respect to your superior, son.
Trespassing on my property and stealing . . .
If I's in your place, I'd be trying hard
to get on my good side. Are you deef and dumb?"
Still, Midnight held his peace. The preacher swung,
buried a fist deep in the black man's belly,
so deep, he felt as if his hand were stuck
in the mysterious gum of guts and soul
and pitchy flesh the mystic was to him.
Mister Midnight staggered but straightened up,
his eyes like bulging bubbles of highway tar,
and dug into his pocket for a fistful
of crimson goopher dust. He let it loose
like devilish cremains on the hot gust.

Brother Abbot stomps Midnight
through the earth's mush way down deep
into the water supply my my

The boys come floatin from the woods
Said the boys come a-floatin on out of the woods
sportin ball caps crooked on top of white hoods

They're ridin supersonic electronic zebras
jailbird stripes throbbin with bass

and the boys go to flowin
"Even as a crack fiend Mama
you always was a black queen Mama"

Beep beep
It's Motorist Rodney King
He roars up on a John Deere tractor
with a sign sayin
VOTE OBAMA
CLINTON (GEORGE) FOR VEEP
SIC 'EM ON OSAMA
Then Motorist hollers
"See ya lizzle alligizzle"

A mattress flies by
with a white woman on it
willin lips spillin syllables of ecstasy
legs spread to a black man
sinewed like a dark-bark crepe myrtle tree
from all that field work
and in the heat of tuppin tuppin tuppin
she looks at Brother Abbot
and whispers
"Poor white you"

"Here," the old man said. His grandson parked the wheelchair. "They was a row through here where Daddy always planted watermelons, in amongst the cotton. Thataway, when you was picking, you could bust open a cool rind and snatch the heart out."

EVERYDAY LOW PRICES, boasted the employees' vests. The old man said, "Jesus in a blue sedan! Muscadines, four dollars a quart. Used to, you could pick them here by the dishpansful. Fresh and free. I told myself I'd never darken the door of this place."

"How come you to change your mind?"

"When you're dying, the hard things you been putting off seem like the only things worth doing."

"You mean coming here or forgiving yourself for selling the land?"

Rubbing an arrowhead between his thumb and forefinger, the old man mumbled, "Bust me open."

Sweet home Ala

LARRY TO AUTOMOTIVES PLEASE
LARRY TO AUTOMOTIVES

so blue

When Grandpa Brownderville was eight years old,
a fellow schoolboy made a rhyme about him:

Herbert Brownderville
Went up a hill,
Eat a pill,
And sound like a bloomin' wheenwhaw.

(As for what a *wheenwhaw* is or what
one sounds like, your guess is as good as mine.)

Whenever this kid saw Grandpa, he would say
the rhyme and snicker. One day on the playground,
Grandpa tackled him and whipped a knife out,
but classmates broke it up.

Fast-forward thirty years—Grandpa got crossways
with the kids of Menzo Littlejohn, a man
who lived about a half mile down the road.
Menzo had a litter of fourteen children,
and they were constantly at Grandpa's house,
asking for this or that—some bread, some milk,
a jar of jelly, or some butter beans.
For a while Grandpa gave them all they wanted,
but being poor himself, eventually
he learned his alphabet between *m* and *p*.
After that a passel of Menzo's children
would gather nightly in the gravel road
in front of Grandpa's house and sing a taunt
they came up with about the Browndervilles.
They'd sing, giggle a little, then sing some more.

Grandpa endured these devilish carolers
for two weeks straight, but then one night at supper,
he blew up like a dynamited stump.
While fourteen Littlejohns twanged in the moonlight,
Grandpa clanged a fork down on his plate
of dog bread, crowder peas, and wilted lettuce
and left the table. In a couple minutes,
returning with a twelve-gauge long-tongue shotgun,
he kicked the screen door open, aimed two feet
or so above his serenaders' heads,
and peppered them with bird shot, man-made hail.
They sprinted homeward, loud across the rocks,
and so our band of country bards was beaten.

Well, sort of. Gunfire ran the singers off,
but what about the song? That was better
than forty years ago and to this day,
at nearly all our cookouts, a grinning uncle
rips open a watermelon, say, or scoops
a hissing patty off the grill and leads
us in that raucous backwoods classic:

Get a box of poison pills
For them crazy Browndervilles.
Kill 'em all! Kill 'em all! Kill 'em all!

HOLY GHOST MAN

1

I met Jack Langston, Ozark preacher
with a watchdog's bark and a stray dog's eyes,
when he was sixty and I was twelve.
In his tryout service at our church,

he said, "I'd like to sing a special."
The piano woman chirped, "You name it."
" 'One Day I Will,' " he said. "About the key of G."
He planted his feet wide

as the band played an intro. Mic drawn at his hip,
he waited like an Old West gunslinger,
ready to meet Sin in the street.
Then he wailed with mountain soul.

Langston's second Sunday with us,
my back-pew buddy said,
"I can't make up my mind about his singing.
It's either great or absolutely awful."

If Langston cried, "Brother Greg, sing me happy!"
I stood beside that old pecan piano, gripped a mic,
and belted out a simple tune,
most often something slow.

In his chair the preacher leaned back—
hands raised, eyes closed—and yielded up
a Halloween moan. Like a low steel note, it rose
and trembled, bending, almost blending with my song.

Always, though Langston could have called
on any of many bird-lunged women,
messy mine was the voice he wanted
haunting his from above.

I could see, as well as hear, our harmony,
my part like a bare bulb
flickering a halo
over a poor man's pecky table.

Our best duet, the two of us agreed,
was "This Is Just What Heaven Means to Me."
Sometimes, partway through the line
When they crown him Lord of all,

I'll be there, Langston yelled,
"I don't know about you,
but this old boy's gonna BE there!"
and shook his loose jowls like a hound.

2

"When God was calling me to preach,"
I once heard Brother Langston say,
"he showed me a vision of a cross
with musical notes floating around it.
I've seen more people saved
through my singing than my preaching."

3

As Langston's trusty music man,
I helped him work revivals.
We set the Delta shouting with our voices,

my guitar, and a black leather book,
its pages edged with gilt and weird of word.

When Brother Langston held his Bible high
and shook it for joy,
it flopped and shined
like a boy's first trout, thumbed proudly in the mouth
and shimmering in the sun.

We ministered in Marvell for a week,
and as we sang "Joshua" on Thursday night,
a woman in the back pew
broke out a tambourine
and stood up all ajangle.

She led a line of shouters
round the sanctuary in a stroll
they called "The Jericho March."
Seven laps and not a wall came down,
but women's hair unbunned itself in waves.

4

Because Langston let out a gruff *hah*
after almost every phrase he preached,
people said he had "the Pentecostal croup."
My mother, praising his athletic pulpiteering,
said, "That man can shuck the corn."
He worked the magic of words—the soul his favorite story.
During Langston's reign
our church became a soul-saving station.
He knew how
to throw a devil-chasing, sin-erasing hallelujah hoedown.

Before he burst into sermon, he always said
a prayer aloud, something like . . .

Heavenly Father, in the special, marvelous, holy name of Jesus,
let the mighty Holy Ghost power come down in this service:
open the windows of heaven, look down with thy divine, sunny face,
and dump a bucketful of honey on our souls.
We'll give you the praise for it in Jesus' name. Amen.

Then it was time for the text:

Flip over to Mark, the tenth chapter, hallelujah,
beginning at verse forty-six . . .

5

Brother Langston liked to say, "Don't complain you came to church
and didn't feel God's presence. Bring God with you."

Also: "Break your plate."
Translation: do some fasting.

Bartimaeus had sat by the wayside begging day in and day out,
but one day he heard a commotion coming down the road, hallelujah,
and he asked who it was and they told him it was Jesus.
He immediately begin to cry out, "Jesus, thou son of David, have mercy on me!"

Folks, it don't do any good to call on Jesus for anything
if you don't have any faith.
He that cometh to God must believe that he is
and that he is a rewarder of them that diligently seek him.
That's why it's so hard for us to touch the Lord,
that's why it's so hard to receive healing anymore:

we don't have faith, hallelujah,
we don't have presistence, praise God,
we don't mean it half the time when we pray,
we whisper a little ole feeble prayer,
it don't go any higher than the top of our head . . .

6

One Sunday night, before service,
I snuck behind the churchyard levee.
My wing tips squished through the glop of the swamp.
Trembly on account of all the fasting I was doing,
I heard my mind call the moon "a cold dish a puddn."
I dipped my finger in it. I licked my finger.
Many mosquitoes, ticklish to my face, neck, and arms,
jiggered in the air. I felt one in my mouth and spat it out.
Imagining a pack of crumbly crackers in my mother's purse,
I went into a trance, but a horsefly buzzed my ear
like a hair trimmer, waking me to myself.
Lips aquiver with the Spirit, I crept into a tall, itchy stand
of indigo and coffee bean to eavesdrop on the preacher.
Across the levee he stood alone beneath a greybeard cypress tree
and prayed for "a great move of God."

7

One time in my own life
I got to the place,
it looked like my ministry was over with, hallelujah.
I couldn't walk across the floor without setting down
before I got halfway across it.
I was so short of breath,
I couldn't even talk above a whisper.

But O praise God, one night in service,
as I was going to pray for a man
(I had already begin to hurt; my lungs was burning),
I just raised my hands and said,
"Lord, you know I can't pray for him."
And something warm touched the tip of my fingers,
settled down through my hands,
all down through my wrists.
I felt it as it touched the top of my head
and slowly settled down.
That warmth went through.

Slowly.

Aw hallelujah to God,
the moment it went through my lungs, I let out a war hoop
to the top of my voice,
and I've been preaching ever since.

O how can you sit still if you're feeling what I feel? . . .

8

One Sunday, while Dad and I were tuning our guitars,
the preacher moseyed over to greet us.
Dad said he had learned a shaving trick that morning:
"If you run the razor sideways cross your neck,"
he claimed, "the hair'll cut a whole lot better."
Langston grumbled, "I hate shaving.
A blade to a man's throat shouldn't orta be all gingerlike.
Shaving's good practice for not taking the world serious.
I tell you, we've domesticated death. Tamed it to a pet.
That's how come it doesn't keep men honest anymore."

9

O hallelujah, folks, listen to me:
It's time to pray and seek the face of God,
Bartimaeus-style!
If you have needs in your life,
get down to business with the Lord
and quit playing church, quit dillydallying around.
Get excited about God!
One man told me he just wasn't the excited kind,
but the very next night, I saw him at the football field
a-hollering and a-jumping like some fool on a Toyota commercial.

Too many so-called Christians are living off a touch
the Spirit gave them twenty, thirty, forty years ago.
"Well, bless God," I've heard them say,
"I got the Holy Ghost when I's in grade school."
Do you still have it? That's what I want to know.
Or are you sitting on the stools of do-nothing?
Folks, we need that Holy Ghost power fresh in our lives.
We need to get all we can and can all we get . . .

10

Langston preached against the evils of TV,
but he sure knew how to work a remote.
He even bought a satellite dish.
(One time, visiting our family, he mentioned
an episode of the *Geraldo* show.)
His favorite things to watch
were Arkansas Razorback basketball and football.
Sometimes during service, if a game was on TV or radio,
he'd have Sister Langston slip next door to the parsonage
and check the score. The man would give us
halftime updates from the pulpit.

11

I know I preach it hard, folks.
You should have heard me when I was young.
I preached hell so hot they could smell the smoke.
But listen, saints: You don't need a preacher to tickle your ear.
You need a preacher to speak the Word.
These young preachers today want to make everything easy.
They think they can update the Gospel and update Jesus.
They want to call his name Dude.
Well, I'm telling you this morning, hallelujah,
the Word of God don't need updating.
It was good for Paul and Silas, and it's good for you and me.
I'm not here to sugarcoat the Word and tell you everything's all right.
Everything's not all right.
The hearts of men are sick with sin, the universe acrumble.
If this nation gets much worse,
God's gonna have to apologize to Sodom and Gomorrah.
America's blinder than Bartimaeus and don't even know it.
I tell you: kill the flesh, smite it with the jawbone of an ass!

What's the matter, church?
You look like you just got hit in the face with a wet squirrel . . .

12

At dusk, under an orgy of sycamore limbs,
a lewd tangle of lovers
God had turned to wood and bleached with moon,
I often sat swapping words with local mojo men.
Their talk made me curious
about women, witchery, and the blues.
I swigged the weird men's whiskey,
which, mixed with guilt, gave me bad dreams.

In one I spied somebody standing at the washtub.
The long hair made me think it was Mama,
but then I saw the beard: Jesus, all frowns,
was rubbing something over a board sudsy with lye.
It was my soul, like a nightgown
some mechanic had been using for a shop rag.
All the other souls,
hung between the clothesline crosses,
danced in the wind like jolly bumpkins at the jamboree,
but Jesus couldn't get mine clean.

I kept sycamoring with the mojo men.
Fascinated by their talk
of dead Delta bluesman Peetie Wheatstraw,
eternally wed, so they swore, to the Devil's daughter,
I felt a gnawing need to hear his music.
After calling a million record stores to no avail,
I tried a place in Little Rock
and got a salesgirl named Eliska (eh-LEASH-kuh).
"Hello, ma'am," I said. "Do y'all have any Peetie Wheatstraw?"

"Step down!" she all but yelled. "The other night
I'm playing Peetie Wheatstraw record
in my friends' house and nobody know him who are you?"
"I'm Greg," I said. "Who are you?"
Right there on the phone,
Eliska—a college senior from the Czech Republic,
in Arkansas to study Southern folkways—
invited me to a party out in the world.

Jesus kept washing, and I kept sinning.

13

The other day, I was driving down the road
with Sister Langston, just easing along, looking at the crops,
and all of a sudden, glory to God,
she looked over at me
and said, "Jack, you 'member when we was young?
We always sat so close together in the truck,
our feelings towards each other was so tender.
And now look at us—
you're way on one side and I'm on the other."
I just turned to her and said,
"Honey, I ain't the one that scooted over."

Saints, hear me and hear me good:
If you ain't as close to God as you once were,
he ain't the one that scooted over.
If you're backslid, it ain't God's fault.
You need to wake up like the prodigal son.
He was wallering in the muck like any common hog.
O but one day he come to his self.
He realized it wasn't any need in him a-living thataway,
feeding on slop when he could eat the fatted calf at his father's table.
Praise God forevermore!
It's time to drop the pail, jump the rail, and hit the trail . . .

14

Langston seldom made eye contact with anyone,
and often talked about—not to—a person in his presence.
At potluck once, his wife chastised him
for eating too much flathead catfish.
He looked down at the many bones strewn across his plate
and said, "She's the criticalest old woman I ever did see."

15

Like the song says, reach out and touch the Lord as he goes by.
Listen to me this morning: Don't wait till it's too late.
O I can hear it thunder even now.
It sounds like the Devil laughing from deep down in his gut.
I can close my eyes and see the storm clouds
boiling on the horizon:
black-ominous! terrible! clouds of despair!
Without the power of God in your life,
you can't stand up to the Devil.
It won't do any good to run away when old Slue-Foot rides in.
He'll lasso you with a tornado and drag you back to hell
so his demon sons can eat your soul for supper.
You need a different wind in your life, O that mighty rushing wind of old.
The Holy Ghost is a holy gust. Saints of God, hallelujah,
let it blow you smooth away!

To get those high winds going, church,
it takes a heap of praying, takes a heap of hard work,
but it's a privilege to work for Jesus.
He'll always have something for us to do.
Even in heaven, hallelujah.
But WOE to those that don't make it in!
They're gonna have something to do, too.
They're gonna be begging for a little drop of water
or wandering around, looking for a cool spot.
Friend, you think it's hot out there right now?
Wait till you see hell.

You say, "Well, Preacher, I didn't know I was going."
Do you know you're not a-going?
There's so-called holy women
with long hair, long sleeves, long dresses,
and tongues so long they could lick peanuts up off the ground.

My hunting buddy told me one old gal
got sloppy drunk one Saturday night
and staggered out of the tavern at one A.M.,
singing "Pyre in the Blood" down the streets of town.
Next day, she come to church shouting like she owned the place—
all spooky cries and fluttery fingers and raised hands,
just like you or me.
At first, I thought she was doing woo pig sooie.
It's a fine line, I reckon.

16

Eliska liked to play me movies at her place.
The summer night we'd set aside for *Baby Doll,*
I arrived on time and rapped at her door.
"It's unlocked," she said, so I showed myself inside,
stepped across a floor colorful with dirty dresses,
and sat down on the couch alone.
Oddly, the film was already playing, halfway through.
Eliska sang in the bathroom,
her voice a quavery soprano.

A few minutes later, she appeared, shower-shiny.
I stood to say hi, startled to find her in only a robe.
She reached up to scrunch her damp hair,
then, grabbing the remote, said, "I'm bored of movies."
The screen went blank and mute.
Eliska drew near,
took hold of a terry dangle at her waist,
and held it out—
to my green eyes, an albino viper's head.
I was frightened and enticed.
"Undo me," she said.
We had never even kissed.

She sounded sure,
but her bashful eyes were twitchy as finches' necks;
they were restless fishes finned with lashes;
homemade animation
coming
choppily to
life
as though an unseen, crayon-wanded child magician
thumbed a deck of drawings;
they were all things dear and busy;
this, and so much more . . .

"Undo me," she said again.
I obeyed. Her cotton robe fell,
became a snowdrift on the floor.
Together, her snowy body, red hair, and green eyes
put me in the Christmas spirit.
She stood still
and let my hands—I thought of them as sleds—
adventure high and low
among rolling white hills
of woman-scape.
The image hologrammed:
I dreamed myself a blind artist
reading the manifold Eliska
with my studious fingers,
but my reading was writing.
There I stood, a boy of seventeen
with a woman bare and beautiful
offering me the mountain,
not the poem that took its place.
Did making metaphors
bring me closer to the tenor,
or shield me from its power?
Eliska kissed me backward, bedward—

tackled me tenderly and blessed my mind
with such a deep, snowy hush,
I heard no thoughts of snow.

A few days later, I asked Langston
how to fight temptations of the flesh.
He said, "Go out to the cemetery
and flash you some naked-woman pictures at a gravestone,
call it all kind of names, cuss its mama,
offer it a beer, do whatever you want—
I bet it won't react.
That's exactly what you got to be, Brother Greg.
Dead.
When the old man is dead, the spirit lives free."

17

If we 'umble ourselves and pray,
if we're presistent, hallelujah,
God will heed our cry.
I come up here every morning and pray for this church,
pray for my ministry,
pray for the leading of the Spirit.
I couldn't preach a lick in the road if I didn't pray, glory to God.
I said I couldn't preach a lick in the road.
I don't have any education to know how to preach.
All I can do is tell you what the Lord tells me.

You see, my Bible says as many as are led by the Spirit of God,
they are the sons of God,
and I found out a long time ago, I was more than a servant:
I was a son. O hallelujah. I said I'm a son of God!
I was led to this place by the Spirit
to be a pastor of this church.
O and I'm glad y'all wanted me to come by, praise God.

I have enjoyed this thing! And I'm still enjoying it!
And I intend to go on praying,
letting the Spirit lead me . . .

I rose one morning in the blue before the sun
and pedaled my Schwinn toward the church.
The red-winged blackbirds got after me.
Guns were popping way off in the woods—
my buddies hunting geese.

Three-quarters of a mile and I was there.
Brother Langston wasn't expecting me.
As I walked up to the door, I could hear him crying out,
every word a bullet in the Devil.
I stepped inside.
The preacher's face wild with stubble,
he looked me in the eye, didn't greet me, didn't run me off.
A second later, he was back to his rebuking,
traipsing up and down those aisles.
Together, we laid hands on the pews
and the piano, the altar benches and the pulpit.
I started rubbing blessing oil on everything in sight.
Any demons who dared fly in our range
were going to wish they hadn't.
Something came over me. I shouted,
"This ground is posted, purple with the blood
of the nail-scarred King of Kings! Angel of Death, pass by!"
Langston hollered glory, and the morning sun
gonged against the windowpanes.

18

At her request I took Eliska to my church.
She wore a scant, silver piece
of postmodern pointiness,

and I overheard an elder say to Langston,
"Brother Greg's lady friend
looks like a hooker from the future."
I skipped the next few services for spite.

Meantime, Eliska got me tipsy twice
and read to me from grimoires.
We did white magic—rituals of the pentagram.
We sang along to Peetie Wheatstraw.
She cast a love spell on us, wood-witch–style,
by tying my left ankle to her right
with nine of her long red hairs.

The preacher called me in a panic,
making sure my lady friend and I had not
"eloped to outer space."

19

Naked and sweaty beside me in bed,
Eliska kicked off her red-and-white covers
like a mall-weary Santa shedding his costume.
"You're a poet," she said,
"but you never write me poetries."

"Does that bother you?"

"I think it maybe does. It definitely does."

"I'll write you a poem."

"No."

"There's a way to take it as a compliment."

"Take what as a compliment?"

"That I haven't written you any poems.
I tried to explain it six months ago, but didn't know how.
That first night we were together together,
poetry was happening in my head like crazy.
I was just scared, wrapping you up in metaphors.
I wasn't even seeing you; I was only seeing poetry."

"But I been thinking at this.
You know when bluesman play a slide,
how he never be still on the note?
He got a hand like hummingbird,
and the note's like some secret humming-heart.
But the guitar's making all that gorgeous racket, right?
So the song's the only realishness,
not the pure, perfect note you can't prove
nor the wire and wood you can.

That's why we need to break it up.
I feel so . . . mysteryless with you.
Like beer-sticky guitar for boring cover band."
Eliska gone, eight years gone,
I think I understand: she wanted
the wettening eye of a poet
to help her blur in two like a midnight moon
so she could dance between
body and myth, between world and word,
at either's fingertips forever.

20

Langston, Dad, and two more men—
Sherman Taylor (seventy-six years tough)
and Robert Hooks—wore sawdust for six months,

building us a new church in town
with their own hands and hammers.
The preacher gave eight grand,
and himself a permanent pay cut.
In August of '97, when the doors opened,
folks desired a season of celebration,
but Langston kept breathing both his favorite fires,
the Holy Ghost and hell.

After our first two services in town,
I left for a year of college overseas.
During my time away, or so the rumor runs,
a few ladies at a church bake sale agreed that Langston
"ought to stop flogging everybody with his Bible all the time."
One woman stood mute and later tattled to the preacher.
Next Sunday, Langston (who loved cotton country,
groused about "rude Yankee squatters up home")
told a congregation he had led for more than half a decade,
"My work ain't appreciated here.
I'm going back home to the hills and retire."

21

One June a few years later, the mojo men
let me join their tabernacle. Out among the cypress knees,
those eerie swamp stalagmites,
we did a drumming ritual and I went into a tizzy.
Ghede, god of sex and the graveyard, possessed me,
announced himself my master of the head.
Afterward, I didn't remember a thing.
They said I was dancing in the mud,
picking wild peppers, and rubbing them in my eyes.

That summer, Brother Langston phoned me.
The caller ID said Baxter Regional Medical Center.

In the year since we had spoken, his voice
had grown frail. When I asked about his health,
he changed the subject: "I hear you're laying out of church."
I didn't respond. He said the soul
was all that mattered, and asked if I had backslid.
I stammered, trying to explain without explaining.
He wept into the phone and said, "I won't let you go."

22

The other evening, I was out watering tomatoes,
my mind stayed on Bartimaeus, and all of a sudden,
I went blind as a bat. When my eyes were opened,
I seen a vision of God's people
stranded in the night, hallelujah,
lightning bugs everywhere like stars a-coming unfixed.
The moon was glowing, and a wind got up in the thorn tree.
I seen angels who their wings were scrolls,
and the scrolls were telling you and me
we better be ready when the storm blows in—
prayed up, packed up, and ready to go up . . .

23

The old man is dead.
Dozens drove up from the Delta for the funeral.
I recall an organ note
urgent as a TV weather warning.

Jack Langston was an Ozark preacher
with a watchdog's bark but a stray dog's eyes.
I hope he jangled up to Jesus in a spaceship tambourine,
singing "I'll Fly Away" loud with mountain soul.

Some days, I go dreaming in the wishing woods
and gambol where the yes-apples redden.
Eliska perches naked on my shoulders.
Nest-warm against my nape, she plucks and sings
while I admire the smooth moon sculpture of her legs.
It's a bluebird day. A fish fry in a clearing.
Langston, his lawn chair saggy in the seat
with faded green unravelment, laughs and gabs,
eating flathead Peter netted, Jacob breaded.
Out of everywhere
a Razorback-quarterback-demoniac—
proud to be a Hog—raids the party,
running zigzag through the weeds, oinking, slobbering.
His ball a jumbo sweet pecan, Hogman hurls a Hail Mary,
and the wobbling oval hatches water moccasins.
Behold, they float our way, treble-cleffing in the air.
Eliska catches one—splat—on a staff she stole from Moses.
In her starry hands menace turns to music:
homemade Gospel—sloppily superb,
a little out of tune, trying to get in time.
The touchdown balloons are rising red suns.
Hallelujah! Woo pig sooie!
Langston puts his Hog hat on John the Revelator.

Down here, all across the countryside,
church window fans with blades like dingy lotus petals
huff hard as though the Holy Ghost were short of breath.
Meanwhile, tornadoes roar, drilling night to bits,
and in hackly towns that look about the same before
as after a twister hits, we keep giving news crews
the freight train simile as if no one ever had.
We wade the latest storm's debris—
bent Polaroid pictures, a broken plate,
a TV antenna discarded like a catfish bone—
and pray our friends across the field aren't hurt, or worse.

You won't catch me with a guitar in the graveyard,
pleading with a stone: "Take the lead. Sing me happy."
Too much work to do.

I'm out to make my life a simple yes,
but to a complicated question.
Yes to the loveliness of sacrifice, to soul,
to disciplined devotion, Langston-style,
but also to the twitchy necks of finches.
To the Devil's Son-in-Law on a Saturday night, yes.
To a shop rag complete with stubborn stains, yes.
Yes to braying "Power in the Blood" down the main drag
at all hours if you fucking feel like it.
Yes to sycamoring.
Yes to a life, down to the last silver dollar moon,
spent in service—not to Langston's law, however,
nor to the bliss of breaking it, but to Eliska's dance,
to song the only realishness.

At my beloved pastor's burial,
I peered across a gravel road
and thought I saw a field white with cotton—
a trick of the eye. The geese rose
as we laid an honorary Deltan in the dirt,
the air alive with wings
like a screen gone to snow.

THE MYSTERIOUS BAR-B-Q GRILL OF
TURKEY SCRATCH, ARKANSAS

Picture a gas tank rigged up as a grill
and mounted on a push mower. Cole saw
it aiming at the road—black, mean, and mobile
like a homemade cannon for a country feud.
His grandpa'd left it to his Uncle Bill,
who grinned, "Daddy's contraption makes me feel
sorta white trash, but surely one of y'all
will keep it, Sam." Sam passed it off on Ray,
who kept it. Bill and Sam dropped graveyard dead
in days, and one time Ray fell gravely ill
himself when someone borrowed it for a day.
After that Ray said, "Man, I'm plumb afraid
to store it in the backyard or the shed.
It's smack-dab in the front or it gets mad."

Home for Thanksgiving, Cole had come to see
his Uncle Ray. As he parked, he thought, *I may
just move home, rent some lakeside property.*
He'd savored the bright blur of his college years,
music, museums, the dash and zoom of the city.
Now Turkey Scratch felt like the fantasy—
one church, one bait shop, a blink on the highway
as he drove south to the deerwoods. He stepped out,
remembering childhood's vertical frontiers,
hours dreaming in the arms of the pawpaw tree.
As a small boy he'd peeled the pale green fruit
and finger-painted the rough trunk in smears
of creamy yellow flesh he used in beers
and puddings not sold at the grocery stores.

When Cole was still in high school, Ray had quit
the farm and gone to work at Farm Bureau
as a claims specialist. Since then he'd cut
the pawpaw down and made Aunt Essie happy
by adding on a new wing where the fruit
once fell. No more did dominickers strut
about as if they owned the place, and now
the yard resembled Astroturf, though once
it doubled as a basketball court, nappy
from the glad slaps of tennies and bare feet.
Some Christmas lights were strung, but not the ones
that Cole remembered—multicolored, gappy
fire hazards. He would miss the canopy
of pawpaw leaves and Essie's mangy puppy.

They'd thrown some killer cookouts on that lawn.
Ray would say, "Go 'head on and get you a bite!"
Cole could still see it, meat loose on the bone
and charcoal smoldering like hearts in jail.
The tire-swing exclamation mark was gone,
but the images had never needed one . . .
There's time within time, many thens inside
one now. The fireflies blow like neon snow
forever, a boy ghosts through a dirt devil
in every joy of your imagination.
Go love the world, the past's a future ago.
Whatever fruit, whatever fire, you'll feel
us meaning in the middle of it all.
We're yours. A pawpaw tree. A homemade grill.

Notes

"Honey Behind the Sun" was triggered by a couple of lines from a Muddy Waters song titled "Louisiana Blues":

I'm going down in New Orleans
Honey behind the sun

"Mawu Names Her Chief Assistant": In the mythology of Benin (formerly known as Dahomey), Legba is the god of the crossroads and a son of the most powerful deity, the goddess Mawu. Legba, one of the best-known trickster gods of West African mythology, embodies the point of contact between the visible and invisible worlds.

"All of This Only Fifty Miles from the Former Home of L. Frank Baum, Creator of *The Wonderful Wizard of Oz*": This poem is based on an interview I conducted with Sharon Weron.

"The Love Song of Jephthah's Daughter" takes its dramatic situation from the eleventh chapter of the book of Judges. Jephthah, a judge over Israel, swears to Yahweh that if he grants him military victory over the Ammonites, he will sacrifice whatever or whoever first emerges from his house when he returns to Gilead. Upon Jephthah's return his only child comes out of the house, dancing and playing a tambourine in celebration of her father's triumph. Jephthah and his daughter agree that he must not go back on his promise to the Lord, but she convinces her father to grant her one request: "Let this thing be done for me: let me alone two months, that I may go up and down upon the mountains, and bewail my virginity, I and my fellows" (11:37).

"Sex and Pentecost," "Boy in the Buttonbush," "Little Lotty Knox," and "Panjandrum" are informed by my study of Zimbabwean poetry in the Shona language. In "Boy in the Buttonbush," I employ the *dzaimbwa* meter of Shona tradition.

"Carlo Silvestrini, Child of Sunnyside": The historical context of this fictional sequence is the Italian peonage system that prevailed on Sunnyside Plantation in early-twentieth-century Arkansas. I drew heavily from two sources, conversations with my Italian friends in Arkansas and a book titled *The Delta Italians: Their Pursuit of "The Better Life" and Their Struggle Against Mosquitoes, Floods and Prejudice,* by Paul V. Canonici.

"Arkansas Blacks": The title refers to heirloom apples developed in the Arkansas Ozarks and known for possessing abundant flavor; thick, dark skins; and the capacity to keep through the winter.

"Waking Up in Baghdad": Species of the *Crataegus* genus are difficult to verify with certainty because there are so many and they hybridize mischievously in the wild. Sugarhaw is *Crataegus viridis* or a similar species, perhaps undescribed.